TECHNIQUE IN SINGING

A Program for Singers and Teachers

RICHARD W. HARPSTER

SCHIRMER BOOKS
A Division of Macmillan, Inc.
NEW YORK

Collier Macmillan Publishers
LONDON

For Burton

Schirmer Books
A Division of Macmillan, Inc.
866 Third Avenue, New York, N.Y. 10022

Collier Macmillan Canada, Inc.

Library of Congress Catalog Card Number: 83-20095

Printed in the United States of America

printing number
    3   4   5   6   7   8   9   10

Library of Congress Cataloging in Publication Data

Harpster, Richard W.
    Technique in singing.

    Bibliography: p.
    Includes index.
    1. Singing—Methods. I. Title.
MT825.H34 1984   784.9'3   83-20095
ISBN 0-02-870350-2

Contents

Preface and Acknowledgments

THE MUCH-ADMIRED ARTIST and pedagogue Aksel Schiøtz once characterized the study of singing as a two-staged process. "Singing as an art," he urged, "cannot be approached before the mastery of singing as a skill."* While that little epithet may seem self-evident, I have frequently been witness to the opposite trend in the real world of singing—a tendency among singers and apprentices to succumb to the sly temptation of tasting the sweets of the singing art before digesting the staples of the singing technique. The results of such vocal malnutrition can be devastating.

Fortunately for this singer, they were not. It was my own serendipity to be led to the studio of the esteemed pedagogue Burton Garlinghouse. From Mr. Garlinghouse, whose rigorous instruction helped me form the ideas and exercises projected in this text, I learned not only how to sing properly, but, happily, how to impart my knowledge of correct singing as well.

This is, as I have implied, a book about vocal skill. It is a distillation of the knowledge, and methods of communicating that knowledge, which I have gleaned from many years of classroom and private instruction in California, New York, and Vienna.

Singer and teacher are this book's audience; classroom and studio are its *mise-en-scène*. However, the syllabus to be presented is in no sense a scenario to be slavishly followed. On the contrary, it is offered as a design for development.

Clearly my debt to Mr. Garlinghouse is immeasurable. I have by no means lost sight, though, of the debt I owe to Miss Eva Gustavson, Mr. Jerald Shepherd, and Mr. Roderick Mount—the kind of loving teachers whose magnanimous contributions to

The Singer and His Art (London: Hamilton, 1970), p. 17.

the art of pedagogy are, regretfully, too infrequently mentioned.

This program also bows to the authority of Ingolf Dahl, Karl Trump, and William Vennard—all men of eminence on whose ears, sadly, my belated acknowledgment falls like the proverbial tree in the forest.

I wish further to applaud the editorial gifts and Job-like patience of Dr. David Greene, without whose refinement the correspondence between image and word—between concept and definition—would have remained askew. My sincere appreciation also extends to Mr. David Ketchum, whose splendid imagination and calligraphic finesse added not only clarity but vitality to the text illustrations.

If *Technique in Singing* is in any way an aid to the teacher, I shall be delighted. If by any means it rescues a struggling apprentice from the quagmire of vocal quackery, I shall be overjoyed.

Richard W. Harpster
Austin, Texas
May 1982

Chapter 1

Introduction

Singing is just this: Space, Freedom, *and* Energy.
—Burton Garlinghouse

ONE SUNNY SUMMER MORNING in Kent, Ohio, after struggling with my own perspectives on voice teaching, I was given a solution in a lecture delivered by the dean of vocal pedagogy, Burton Garlinghouse. At the core of his lessons was the discourse given that day, a synoptical review of the three schools of vocal pedagogy: *bel canto, psychological-imagery,* and *mechanistic.*

It is that definitive summary (and many reinforcements in the studio) which frame the program for vocal development you are about to study. It would be wise at this point, then, to become acquainted with the vocabulary and concepts of these three schools, drawing parallels and distinctions.

The *bel canto* (It "beautiful singing") school flourished in the eighteenth century, primarily in Italy, and was carried on into the twentieth century by such artists as Caruso and Gigli. Its most widely recognized attribute is its emphasis on *legato* singing.

1

Relying heavily on metaphor and psychological suggestions, the psychological-imagery school is audible in modern pedagogy in such remarks as "darken the vowel" and "drink in the tone."

Alongside a renewed interest in empirical science, the mechanistic approach arose in the mid-1800s as a response to anatomical and acoustical curiosity. Its contribution to our understanding of vocal resonance is considerable. In contrast to the more "subjective" psychological-imagery approach, the mechanistic school might be regarded as the "objective" approach.

While each school obviously differs in terms of language and philosophy, all three concur that the art of producing, maintaining, and coloring a sung line can be reduced to three primary functions: *posture and breathing, registration,* and *resonation.*

Posture and breathing techniques center on the correct positioning of the body, tension-reducing exercises in posture, inhalation and exhalation skills, tone production, practical methods of attack and release, and the goal of all breathing excellence, the legato line.

Registration deals with the control of register adjustments (the manipulations of the "heavy" and "light" mechanisms), variance of vowel colors (known as *covering* and *focusing*), and the training of the bridging area called the *passaggio.*

Resonation involves the development of vowel resonance and "placement," good tone quality and "projection," and ways of maintaining the "large throat."

In order to communicate its ideas about these three functions, each school developed its own distinctive vocabulary. Table 1.1, whose source is the lecture discussed above, is a synopsis of the schools and their respective terminology. It serves as the foundation on which the following chapters rest.

Scanning this synopsis quickly verifies that no matter which school a pedagogue adheres to, the goal for all good teachers in singing is threefold: energy, freedom, and space.

It is not too soon for you, students and teachers, to begin drawing freely from all three schools of thought. You will find that the choice of terminology and approach is often determined by the psychological makeup of the student and singer, at the moment or in general. Sometimes even the particular mood of the student or teacher will decide which words or concepts will communicate most effectively for that particular lesson.

TABLE 1.1

	Bel Canto	Psych.-Imag.	Mechanistic
Breathing	Sustained sound, legato	"Support," body connection	Posture and breathing
Registration	Agility and flexibility, range	Vocal freedom	Facility in register adjustment
Resonation	"Big tone," "bel canto"	Tone color, tone quality	"Large throat," resonation

Up to this point I have treated singing technique largely as a matter of initiating, sustaining, and amplifying *tone* (and will describe that treatment in Chapters 2–7). But there is more to singing than tone production alone. Tone production means essentially vowel production. But words need consonants to be intelligible. So the correct enunciation of consonants, or articulation, is the subject of the chapter which follows tonal development, Chapter 8.

The correct pronunciation of words, the science of diction, also belongs to the realm of tone and articulation, where words are conceived as vowels (tone) plus consonants (articulation). At the same time, a study of diction acts as the bridge between techniques in singing and skills of interpretation; words once treated as tone and articulation are now regarded as dramatic elements. Chapters 9–12 thus introduce the craft of pronunciation in Italian, French, German, and English, while they prepare the way for the next step in this vocal program: the elusive art known as *interpretation*. In Chapter 13 you will learn about the deeper levels of tone and poem, of music and drama. By delving into a poem or scenario seeking nuance and characterization, you will peel away surface layers of the musical score to find its underlying meanings and symbols.

In the final chapter of this study you will arrive at the peak of your technical ascension with the balancing of vocal skills and the fusion of tone and words. I have coined a neologism to capture the essence of that balancing act in the performance itself: *cantus lībrātus*. I have chosen Latin—at the risk of appearing a snob—because it incorporates all the ramifications of balance as a *dynamic* concept. *Cantus,* for example, means either "song," "singing," or even "musical utterance." *Librātus* implies "suspension" and "dynamic balance." Cantus librātus, then, connotes something akin to singing in a dynamic balance of habits.

You are no doubt a little confused and perhaps more than a little confounded by the scope and vocabulary of this study. I assure you, it is a progressive series of lessons you are about to undergo, a paced program designed for a fifteen-week schedule. It will develop your awareness and skill from the most basic breathing and posture discipline, through the more sophisticated and yet personal methods of intepretation, to the final fruition, cantus librātus.

By following this format—by reading the text, answering the study questions, practicing the exercises and Sieber vocalises,* and analyzing the many suggested recording examples—you, both students and teachers, will develop not only the voice but the ear as well.

I would add that this program will achieve its highest success when practiced in conjunction with studio work or a voice class. In any event, do not try the exercises without some sort of supervision, especially in those cases where caution is advised.

Study Questions and Exercises

1. Memorize the synopsis of pedagogical schools in Table 1.1, even though at this stage that gesture may mean little more to you than an exercise in recall. You will be referring to this format throughout the course of the text.

2. How would a vocalist of the bel canto school describe "space"? "Energy"? "Freedom"? How would a mechanist define these three concepts?

3. Stand in front of a large mirror and watch yourself sing a very comfortable *ah.* Immediately write down your impressions, particularly in reference to posture (neck, jaw, shoulders, chest position, stomach, stance, etc.) and the way you breathe. Repeat several times until you have a thorough list. Be sure to write everything down, no matter how insignificant it may appear to you at this time.

---

* All fourteen chapters are synchronized to Ferdinand Sieber's *36 Eight-Measure Exercises,* Opus 93 (New York: G. Schirmer, 1967).

Chapter 2

Posture and Breathing

We have a right to say that the co-ordination of the singing act commences with the taking of the breath.

—Herbert Witherspoon,
Singing: A Treatise for
Teachers and Students

BEFORE YOU EVER UTTER a single tone you must be in control of a posture which facilitates that utterance. In short, posture either aids or hinders breathing. Posture which aids is characteristic of a singer who

1. *Stands on both feet* with the body weight shifted slightly forward on the balls of the feet, preferably with one foot a little ahead of the other.

2. Stands with *spine erect*, avoiding pressure on the pelvic area.

3. Stands with *chest elevated*, allowing for a sort of "free swing" of the belly, out and in (during the inhale–exhale episode).

4. *Keeps neck muscles relaxed* so that the head can turn easily, as if on a swivel.*

*Cf. de Young, 1958, pp. 46–47; Witherspoon, 1925, p. 55.

Once these four requirements are met, the singer is ready to study the techniques of breathing.

There are three possible ways to breathe. The first, called *clavicular* or *shoulder* breathing, uses only the shoulders to draw in the air. Shoulder breathing is the least desirable method, and should be avoided. Not only does it provide an insufficient supply of air, but it may even lead to neck and throat tension, and it also ruins the posture described above.

Costal or *rib* breathing, which employs the muscles woven about the ribs to inhale, is more desirable than shoulder breathing, but still it is only genuinely efficient when coordinated with the third type, belly breathing.

Belly or *diaphragmatic* breathing is the most effective means of inhaling and exhaling. The technique of belly breathing is based on the scientific principle that when the sheet-like muscle called the diaphragm *lowers,* air is drawn in through the mouth and throat to fill the vacuum created; and when it *raises,* air is thrust out (see Figure 2.1).

If you examine yourself breathing, you will notice that in *inhaling* (diaphragm down) the suction of the air is accompanied by an expansion of the lower ribs and a protrusion of the belly. *Exhaling* (diaphragm ascending) reverses these movements.

Let us take some time out to practice some exercises that will cement your understanding of belly breathing. First, lie face up on the floor, with a slightly heavy object such as a book placed on your stomach. As you inhale (diaphragm down) observe that in

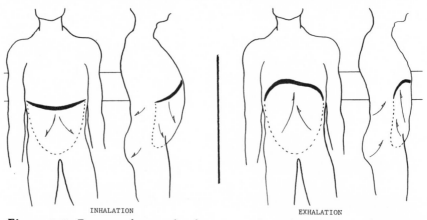

INHALATION   EXHALATION

Figure 2.1. Posture during diaphragmatic breathing. Note position of diaphragm during inhaling (down) and exhalation (up).

expanding the ribs and protruding the belly you raise the book slightly. Now hold that air, not by closing the throat, but by suspending the abdominal area (more about that soon). Now, as if gently blowing out a candle, exhale slowly (diaphragm ascending), observing that the book gradually lowers.

Another method, which sidesteps potential confusion over the "lower" and "raise" indications above, is that of standing against a wall and breathing. Observing the four points of good posture outlined above, stand erect with your back tangent to a wall, and place your right hand flat against the stomach area. Inhale while noting the expansion of the lower ribs and belly (but don't raise your shoulders). Suspend the air. Now exhale, marking the gradual contraction of the belly area. Repeat this exercise in front of a full-length mirror, and do *not* go on until you have mastered the posture and breathing skills presented so far.

Now let us recapitulate the separate elements of inhalation and exhalation.

During *inhalation:*

1. The rib cage enlarges in all directions.
2. The chest is elevated (and expands with the addition of *costal* breathing).
3. The diaphragm contracts and descends, pushing the contents of the abdomen downward and the belly slightly outward.

During *exhalation:*

1. The chest drops and its volume diminishes.
2. The diaphragm ascends to a higher position.
3. The rib cage returns to its normal "at rest" position.

Such is the process of breathing when inhalation and exhalation are statically isolated. But in the dynamic process of respiration in singing, a five-stage operation takes place. For purposes of clarification, let us take each stage out of sequence, define it, and practice it.

Stage 1: Posture check. Elevate the rib cage by folding your hands over your head and maintaining that stance as you drop your hands. With your mouth formed for an *ah* attack, check that the <u>tongue is relaxed and the jaw is loose and not protruded.</u> This is essential. (If you have difficulty with a lower jaw overbite, try blowing into a soda bottle "flute style" and then holding that jaw position.) Make sure that the <u>neck is relaxed</u> ("twirl" it a couple of times to check); the chest is elevated; and that you have a feeling of "<u>verticality,</u>" i.e., <u>a weighty connection from the top of your head to the supporting feet</u> below. Now your whole being is ready for inhalation, which you will execute as if taken by surprise—an "up" sensation.

Stage 2: "Flop" the belly, as if you are "making yourself fat," while still keeping the rib cage elevated.

Stage 3: Expand the lower ribs and costal muscles as you draw in the air by lowering the diaphragm, thus inhaling slowly.

Stage 4: Suspend that air. This technique of <u>suspension,</u> also known as *muscular antagonism* (Vennard, 1967, p. 29) and *balanced retention* (de Young, 1958, p. 45), forms the basis for breath management and support. In psychological-imagery terminology, the sensation of "suspending the air" is that of a floating, <u>buoyant</u> "<u>support,</u>" a feeling of expectation. Think of a buoy floating on rippling water. The <u>bel canto</u> school implies it when it advocates singing "<u>on the breath.</u>" In mechanistic terms, "suspending the air" results from the push-pull action of the muscles between the ribs and surrounding the diaphragm; some muscles pull against the action of certain other muscles. The control of this antagonism prevents any sudden loss of air through an explosive release of air, and can be best conceived, in Schumann-Heink's words, as "budgeting the air."

Pedagogues call it breath management, the ability to balance the supply of air according to the amount of sound and energy required. The ability to keep the sound energetic and yet maintain a certain flexibility is called breath support. For obvious reasons, both depend on the well-developed art of suspension of the air supply, our fourth stage.

Stage 5: Exhale slowly by contracting the abdominal muscles and thus raising the diaphragm.

Before continuing, stop and practice this sequence through, slowly, in front of a mirror. As you practice, keep in mind these do's and don't's:

1. For this and all other exercises found in this text, never go on to the next stage until you have perfected the one you are presently practicing.

2. Don't be alarmed if at first you experience slight dizziness. You have been hyperventilating and simply need to take a short break from the exercise.

3. Never force the air stream in either direction, but let it flow.

4. Begin to imagine the process of breath management early in the first stage, before inhalation, as well as during suspension.

Now repeat the exercise in front of a mirror with this addition: you are going to "attack" on *ah.* An attack is a stroke of the abdomen "in" on an exhalation—or so we will conceive of it at this stage. The sound that results will resemble a *huh.* (Remember to form the vowel first and do not move the jaw.) Musically it is written somewhat as in Example 2.1.

Ex. 2.1

huh   huh   huh

This and the preceding exercises form the foundation for respiration and attack. Now we need to move on to the process of making sound and sustaining it.

Hold your hands in front of you as if you were going to play the piano. Now bring them together so that the sides of the index fingers meet. This is analogous to the way your vocal bands (often referred to as "cords") appear during speech and singing. When air, energized by exhalation, travels from below through the windpipe (trachea) and vibrates your vocal bands (represented here by your hands), sound is produced. That procedure which connects breathing to singing is known as *phonation*. Go through the following six-staged process now, just as you did with the respiration practice—in "slow motion" in front of a mirror:

Stages 1–3: Exactly the same as 1–3 in *respiration*.

Stage 4: The attack. First, play around a little with *ah* as described above. Then, gently, with the proper posture, forming the mouth for *ah*, sing *ah* on any tone selected at random. (And never attack with the throat closed, the so-called "glottal stop.")

Stage 5: The sustained sound, or *sostenuto*. Compare this to the suspension stage in respiration, and review balanced retention. At this stage you sustain your *ah* by means of good breath management and muscular antagonism. It is important that you master sostenuto before undertaking the sophisticated legato singing outlined below. As you approach the point of diminishing air supply, you are at Stage 6.

Stage 6: The release. There are two possibilities here, either the exhale release or the inhale release. For the former simply exhale without phonating (i.e., vibrating the vocal cords). The latter takes some getting used to, especially since you will undoubtedly have a tendency to gag at first. To stop the tone with this approach, inhale through an open throat. In either event, never stop the tone by closing the throat. Rather, let the coordination of the diaphragm and the inhale or exhale release cease the tone.

As you review these two sets of exercises, remember some words of advice and caution:

1. As a general rule, always avoid the glottal stop (in French, the *coup de glotte*), a very sloppy way to start or stop the tone. If you are not sure what the glottal stop sounds like, let our expression *Uh-oh!* serve as an example.

2. Often a slight aspirating *h* sound will accompany your attack on vowels. It is perfectly acceptable so long as the throat is open and the attack is not "high" or "shallow," but "low" in the throat space.

3. Never explode the attack, but use wise breath management to budget the air release.

4. Sostenuto is not a static sound but one full of energy. During sostenuto imagine that you are "drinking in the tone."

5. Always relate your inhaling and exhaling to the *total body* and not just to the local, obvious breathing areas. That is, let that ebbing action touch all your nerve centers (or "chakras" if you are so oriented) while you are *centered* in the solar plexus area. This total body involvement, which seems to connect your feet to the universe, is what the psychological-imagery school means by "body connection."

Now, standing sideways to the mirror, practice the entire attack-release sequence. Look for errors in posture (particularly jaw-related mistakes), inhalation ("gasping," for example, is an indication that the throat is constricted), breath management, and release. Practice both types of release in this exercise. If you are still having trouble with phonation, begin again back at the respiration sequence. When sostenuto skill is secure, go on to legato.

The logical expression of singing sostenuto on one note is the sustained singing from one note to another, or legato. Meaning literally "connected" singing, legato is the foundation of the bel canto technique—and for that matter, of all artistic singing—while it is the reflection of a masterful breathing skill. Think of singing a legato line the way you would a relay race, connecting tones and rests the way the passing of the baton joins the runners. Even when you exhale, you must treat the pause that results as part of the legato line: nothing is static in the beautifully sung line.

Practically, legato is nothing more than sostenuto on different tones. To demonstrate, sing the iteration in Example 2.2 until attack, sustain, and release are all one smooth sequence (men one octave below written):

Ex. 2.2

Immediately follow with these four sustained notes on one breath only (Example 2.3):

Ex. 2.3

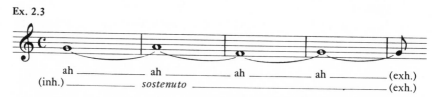

Your first milestone: you have just sung a legato phrase.

Generally speaking, there are three common breathing errors to be avoided. The first is summed up in a word all performers dread: tenseness. Tenseness may be a result of faulty posture. A stiff neck eventually becomes a tense throat. So does a "tight" jaw. If the rib cage is not elevated, the bad breath management that it causes can in turn create throat tenseness. (Obviously, if the rib cage is not elevated, giving a feeling of space in front and around the upper back, then the free in-out swing of good breathing technique will be greatly inhibited as well.)

Or faulty respiration technique can be the culprit. Shoulder breathing and lack of body connection affect breath management and support, and eventually the throat. If the belly is held rigid during the suspension—sometimes referred to as "German" breathing—the tone will sound "driven," and the lack of flow may create stiffness and rigidity, particularly noticeable in the neck and throat. A gasp accompanying inhaling is simply *verboten;* not only does gasping indicate the throat is constricted, it can actually produce dryness in the throat, a serious impediment to freedom in singing.

A second common oversight, in addition to tenseness-causing faults, results from poor breath management: the explosion of air on the initial attack. Besides destroying the legato line, this mistake compounds itself by imparting an often unwanted accent to the initial tone.

It is not possible to exaggerate the damage done by the third breathing error, the infamous *coup de glotte*. Using the throat to substitute for the abdominal and costal muscles in breath control not only strains the throat, but, as Blanche Marchesi (1932, p. 73) warns, "produces the most detrimental effect on the vocal cords themselves [resulting in] swelling, nodes, and paralysis."

In sum, breathing is the essence of singing: if you cannot breathe correctly, you cannot sing correctly.

Respiration can be studied as a five-stage process, the central feature of which is the suspension of the air supply. Phonation can be learned in a similar manner, by practicing a six-stage sequence, the nucleus of which is the art of sustained sound, or sostenuto. Sostenuto skill depends physically on the techniques of balance and antagonism known as breath management and breath support. While breathing gymnastics alone may develop fluency in respiration and phonation, they do little to exercise support skills. Support exercises and the actual singing of songs are the only means to do this.

Finally, the sine qua non of artistic singing—and the logical sequel to sostenuto singing—is legato, a technique of connecting sounds and pauses which relies on a perfected ability in breath management for its success.

Study Questions and Exercises

1. What is wrong with "shoulder breathing"? Why is belly breathing called "diaphragmatic"? Why is it necessary to keep the chest elevated? What is a *coup de glotte* ("glottal stop"), and why should it be avoided?

2. Some singers advocate breathing through the nose rather than through the mouth. What are the advantages and disadvantages of nose breathing? Of mouth breathing? (Think this one over now, but don't try to answer it yet. Wait

until you have reached Chapter 8. Then, while you are practicing your "linguopalatals," the answer should suddenly be clear to you.)

3. What does it mean that breathing is a "dynamic" process?

4. What are the six stages in phonation?

5. *Respiration exercises.* Without phonating, try exercising the breathing mechanism as
   a. *Marcato:*

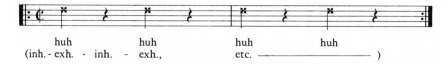

      huh   huh   huh   huh
(inh. - exh. - inh. - exh.,   etc. ───────────)

This will sound similar to a "stage whisper."

   b. *Staccato* (called "dog-pant," exhaling on all attacks):

        huh - huh - huh - huh,   etc. ──────────
       (inh. - exh. - exh. - etc. ────────────────)

6. *Sostenuto exercise.* Practice the following exercise at different starting pitches. Pay careful attention to posture as well as attacks and releases (men sing an octave lower than written):

  [h] Ah ____   [h] Ah ____   [h] Ah __ [h] Ah __   [h] Ah __ (1. inh.)
 (inh. - exh. inh. - exh. - inh., etc.) ──────────────── (2. exh.)

7. *Legato.* Look at the first exercise in Sieber. Sing (always) the *unitalicized syllables:*
   a. As written musically, on the vowels only (*ah, ay, ee, oh, oo*).
   b. As written textually, but on one tone.
   c. As written, being attentive to attacks, releases, and the legato line.

Chapter 3

Breathing and Vowels

The air should flow out in a gossamer filament.
—Richard de Young,
The Singer's Art

THERE IS ONE FUNDAMENTAL ACT in posture that connects breathing with the vowels: the formation of the vowel *before* inhalation. This action simply must become a habit before the singer can proceed unencumbered to the other aspects of breathing in relation to the vowels. Not only does this habit aid in minimizing jaw motion, it also helps to set up a sequence connecting good breathing technique with the art of legato singing. Practice this act on *ah* before a mirror until it becomes a habit. Then go on to the other vowels.

There are five essential, or "primary," vowels: *ah, ay, ee, oh,* and *oo.* Be thinking, even at this early stage, that vowel formation begins really in the throat first, then in the mouth— not vice versa.

Let's begin with *ah* as in *father,* symbolized [ɑ].* Standing in

*Part of the IPA, or International Phonetic Alphabet (see the Appendix). Memorize each symbol as it comes to you in the course of the text, so that by

front of a mirror, note whether the jaw is loose, the tongue relaxed, and the throat very open and spacious (as if you were going to yawn). Now speak or sing [ɑ], coordinating breathing and phonation as you imagine the vowel "high in the head" and sense its sound "forward," or in the region of the nose bridge. *Avoid swallowing or muffling* the vowel, and make sure the mouth is wide enough to fit two fingers inside (B. Marchesi, 1932, p. 3). Now review the six-staged phonation exercise, on [ɑ].

Ay, as in *pay,* symbolized [e], is, as you will observe in Chapters 6–7, a very difficult vowel to control with respect to space and resonance. For now, picture the [e] as halfway between your [ɑ] and the bright *ee* of *knee.* Open your mouth, and do not clinch the jaw; think the throat space of [ɑ] as you say *hay.* Now practice on [e] as you did on [ɑ].

The third primary vowel is the bright *ee,* as in *me* ([i]), which you have just encountered. In Chapters 6–7 you will learn two different ways of phonating on [i]. For now, form the vowel in the same manner as the others, keeping the throat spacious and the jaw loose and rather "tucked in" (to avoid protruding). Round your lips slightly and sense the tone coming from the nose bridge. Now practice the whole phonation sequence on [i] in front of a mirror.

With *oh,* as in *tow* ([o]), the jaw approaches a posture very much like the flute or soda bottle embouchure introduced earlier. As with the other vowels, watch for the bridge sensation, notice how open the throat feels, and think of the tone as being "in the head." Practice phonating on [o] in front of a mirror.

You will find, I am afraid, that it is going to take some effort on your part to conquer the pure *oo* ([u], as in *who*) vowel. For if you are American, I can assure you that your "inner ear" is full of many recorded adulterated [u] forms; more than likely you have been persuaded to substitute *ee-you* or *uh-oh* or even *aah-oh* for the pure *oo.* The vowel [u] resembles [o] in jaw position and throat space. Imagine the tone very "high in the head" even as you note the low position of the "Adam's apple." Make sure that it floats low and free, by the way. Repeat your phonation exercise on [u] in front of a mirror. If you are phonating [u]

---

the time you reach Chapter 13 you will have the entire alphabet learned by heart.

correctly you will see a *v* shape emerging from the center of the upper lip and spreading out to the cheekbones.

At this juncture it would be wise for you to practice all five vowels in a sostenuto succession slowly on one comfortable tone. Be on guard against excessive jaw motion. When you feel reasonably secure with the primary vowels, them move on to the variations of the vowels.

A handy scheme for grasping all the variations of the primary vowels is to classify these five vowels according to their pronunciation as *open* or *closed*. In most of the languages in which we sing, vowels which appear the same often sound quite different. While the *e* in *grey* looks the same as that in *tether*, we know that the former vowel is closed ([e]) and the latter is open ([ɛ]). In foreign languages as well as in English, this distinction between open and closed sounds is often the only means of differentiating word meanings: Consider the ramifications of saying the word *fillings* (open *i*, or [I]) when you really mean to say *feelings* (closed *i*, or [i])!

As you practice the following comparisons, begin to conceive of the difference between open and closed vowels as the difference in mouth and throat space. Thus,

[ɛ] as in *pet* is more open than [e] as in Ger. *Weh*

[I] as in *myth* is more open than [i] as in *weep*

[ʌ] as in *touch* is more open than [o] as in *tone*
    (Ger. *Sonne*)   (Ger. *Sohn*)

[U] as in *took* is more open than [u] as in *tooth**

[Y] as in Ger. *füllen* is more open than [y] as in Ger. *fühlen*

[œ] as in Ger. *Hölle* is more open than [o] as in Ger. *schöne*

Practice speaking all six sets, first in open–closed order, then the reverse. Be aware of your mouth and throat positions, and remember to round your lips on the vowels after [U].

---

*You may run across listings which differ from my presentation (Vennard, 1967, p. 136, for example). Generally these are graphs designed to clarify vowel resonance, the subject of our Chapter 7. The above scheme aims more at introducing phonetics and pronunciation and facilitating memorization of the IPA.

When the psychological-imagery school speaks of "light" and "dark" tones, it implies another sort of variation scheme, the light-dark, or *chiaroscuro*, contrast. These are variations in vowel color, or *timbre*. Preliminary to learning to color a vowel, heed this word of warning: Never attempt to color a vowel before you are sure your primary vowels are pure. In short, if you cannot sing a pure [u], do not try the variation [y]. The vowels [ɔ], as in *draw*, and [æ], as in *cat*, should be color variations of [ɑ] and not substitutes for it.

For practice in vowel coloring, let us make a few chiaroscuro variations on the five primary vowels. For example, [æ], as in *passion*, and [a], as in *task*, are "brighter" than [ɑ]. Increasingly "darker" than [ɑ] are [ɒ], as in *hot*, and [ɔ], as in *draw*.

[ɛ] may be regarded as less "bright" than the primary vowel [e]. "Darker" variations of [ɛ] are [ɜ], as in *her* (without the r); [ə], as in the first vowel of *perhaps;* and [ɝ], as in *word* (*r* sounded).

The "brightest" vowel, [i], may be "darkened" to [I] (*hit*) and further still darkened to [y] (Ger. *Kyrie, fühlen*).

A pure [o] can be "shaded" as [ʌ] (*son*) or [ø] (Ger. *böse*) and [œ] (*Hölle*).

One line of variations of [u] could be thought of as "German": [u] to [U] (*took*) to [y] (*kühle*) to [Y] (*Müllerin*). Another emanates from [u] to the French [y], as in *lui* and *puissance* (see Chapter 10). (The French [y], incidentally, is formed by combining the pronunciation of *ee* ([i]) with the rounded lips and open throat of *oo* ([u]).)

No doubt, as you contemplate memorizing this entire gamut of vowels and their variations, you are a bit discouraged. "What an impossible task!" you are saying to yourself.

Let me give you some words of comfort. Although the chore of learning the primary vowels and their variations is at first admittedly arduous, think of the rewards: With the perfection of that task you will not only have laid the foundation for your comprehension of the relationship between vowels and resonance, you will also have done the groundwork for the entire discourse on diction and articulation skills presented in Chapters 8–12.

As to *how* I would go about memorizing these vowels and variations, may I suggest that the first step is immediately to memorize the five primary vowels and their corresponding IPA

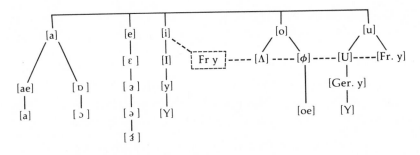

Figure 3.1. Pure vowels and their variations.

symbols. You might even consider making your own list of words to illustrate each symbol.

Then study Figure 3.1. Practice phonating (as in the six-step exercise) on all five primary vowels and their variations. Then memorize the figure as five sets of vowel sounds.

Now take some time to reflect on your achievement at this point. Look what you have already accomplished! You have relearned correct posture and breathing; you can phonate correctly and sustain sound properly; and you have mastered the pure vowels and can vary their color deliberately. That is quite a chunk of technique and a secure basis for everything that is to follow. The next stage in your vocal development is the mastery of the second function in beautiful singing, *registration*.

Study Questions and Exercises

1. Sing the six-tiered sequence of open–closed vowels ([ɛ]–[ø]) sustaining one tone, slowly. Don't forget to check your posture and breathing while you are concentrating on vowel formation and coloring. Take this and other exercises slowly and systematically. Remember that any worthy study of technique is progressive and cumulative: The success of your next step depends largely on the degree of perfection you attain with your present one.

2. On one note sustain the following series, reminding yourself that vowels are formed initially in the throat: [u]–[o]–[ɑ]–[e]–[i]. What do you notice about the throat? The back of the tongue? The nose bridge?

3. Do the same with the sequence [u]–[a]–[i]–[a]–[e]. Describe [i] sensations.

4. Try this one: [u]–[U]–[o]–[ʌ]–[ɔ]–[ɑ]–[a]–[ɛ]–[e]–[i].

5. Look at your Sieber, no. 1. *Speak* the entire four phrases without stopping. Have you noticed yet that all the Sieber exercises derive from one seven-syllable sequence?

6. Now sing this exercise, on one tone, in front of a mirror. You will be criticizing yourself, at this stage, on (1) posture and breathing; (2) sostenuto and legato; and (3) vowel purity skills. Now sing Sieber no. 2 exactly the same way.

7. Sing Sieber nos. 1 and 2 as written, keeping in mind the three sets of criteria of Study Question 6. What is the jaw "doing"? Are you careful on the rests to breathe correctly? Are your [u] sounds pure?

Chapter 4

Registration

A master should endeavor to help the young soprano unite the feigned and the natural voice . . . for if they do not perfectly unite, the voice will be of diverse registers . . . and must completely lose its beauty.
—P. F. Tosi,
Observations on the Florid Song

THE CLASSIC AND LONGSTANDING DEFINITION of registration offered in the nineteenth century by the founding father of modern vocal pedagogy, Manuel Garcia (*Treatise*, p. 4), is still the most complete. "A register," Garcia maintains, is

> a series of consecutive and homogeneous sounds produced by the same mechanical means, and differing essentially from other sounds originating in mechanical means of a different kind; hence it follows that all the sounds belonging to the same register are of the same quality and nature, however great the modification of quality and power they must undergo.

In sum, a register is a series of sounds that (1) match; (2) are produced by the same "mechanism for the creation of sound" (Ruth, 1963, p. 2); and (3) can be differentiated from another such series by the trained musical ear.

There is hardly unanimity among the schools of singing as regards the number and nature of the registers. Vennard (1967, pp. 69–70) has sorted the diverse opinions into three approaches. The "idealistic" approach regards the voice as one register with no "holes" or "breaks" from top to bottom (Witherspoon, 1925, p. 23). In actuality, this one-register concept is the ideal for which all singers strive, even if—according to the outlooks of the other schools—it ignores nature.

The "hypothetical" school, holding to a two-register theory, credits the voice with two octaves of "heavy mechanism" and two octaves of "light mechanism." The two overlap, forming an octave of *voix mixte,* or mixed voice, in the process.

The program in this book belongs to the third school, the three-register approach. Although most students of this philosophy concur on the original "chest–head–falsetto" format for men and "chest–middle–head" outline for women, there are some factions which deviate from the bel canto model. Curiously enough, Garcia reversed the male arrangement, making it "chest–falsetto–head." Some authors, including Shakespeare (the pedagogue, not the bard) and Tetrazzini, preferred the more generalized "chest–medium–head" description. A variation of this scheme is Ruth's "chest–middle–high." And a kind of hybrid form of this and the "hypothetical" approach is the construct preferred by de Young and others, "heavy–middle–light."* My approach is conservative and "realistic," perceiving the three registers as "chest–head–falsetto" and "chest–medium–head" for men and women, respectively.

Let us make sure that we agree on the meaning of the terms of registration before seeking to use those terms to describe its intricate functions (cf. Vennard, 1967, pp. 250–251):

Chest register:	An adjustment producing heavy tones suitable for *forte* singing and for the lower part of the compass.
Coordinated register:	An adjustment having some qualities of both light and heavy registration.
"Covered" register:	An adjustment to the upper part of the male voice, not falsetto.
Crooning:	A style in singing which is light in registration and intensity and depends upon a microphone.

---

*I by no means intend to imply that there is universal acceptance even of the notion of register theory itself. Some teachers, like Lilli Lehmann (1942, pp. 107–111), will not concede that registers even *exist* in nature at all.

Head register:	An adjustment producing light flutelike tones, suitable for soft singing and for the upper part of the compass. The term originally applied to what is now recognized as the woman's light mechanism.
Heavy mechanism:	The laryngeal adjustment in which the vocal bands are thick. The chest voice or full voice.
Middle register:	The register between the chest and falsetto.

In addition, every singer should know the set of definitions referred to as the classification of voice types. According to the broadest division, there are four voice types from highest to lowest: soprano, alto (or contralto), tenor, and bass—two female and two male voices. As you have no doubt surmised from the Sieber collection, these four basic voice types can be expanded to include six concert solo voices: soprano, mezzo-soprano, contralto, tenor, baritone, and bass.

Sopranos, the most popular of the voices, are named not only for their differing qualities but also for the repertoire which suits their respective ranges, qualities, and technical abilities. The most familiar of the three soprano voices is the lyric soprano. In her repertoire you will generally find melodious, very singable arias whose nature is lyric as opposed to dramatic. By contrast the dramatic soprano—that hefty voice we always associate with the operas of Richard Wagner—is a powerful, dramatic voice which generally performs in a heavier adjustment than the lyric soprano. Singing in the highest register of all sopranos—and often without words—is the coloratura soprano. A *colorature* is an embellishment of a melody, an ornament. A coloratura singer and hence soprano is one who specializes in highly ornate arias and songs, in a lighter adjustment than the dramatic soprano.

Mezzo means "half" in Italian. The mezzo-soprano, or "half-soprano," shares the range and qualities of the dramatic soprano, on the one hand, and the contralto, on the other. One of the most famous mezzo roles is Carmen.

The genuine contralto voice is actually rather rare. Being the lowest of the female voices, the contralto is often called upon to sing in the *tessitura* (predominant range) below middle C. The timbre of the contralto voice is much "darker" and even "thicker" than the other female voice types.

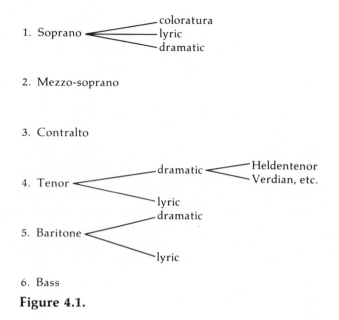

Figure 4.1.

The highest of the male voices is the tenor voice, which has two textures, lyric and dramatic. A lyric tenor is most comfortable when singing long, melodious lines which do not require a consistently heavy mechanism. For example, most Mozart operas and Italian arias written before Verdi suit the lyric tenor. Verdi operas, however, require a heavier voice type than Mozart operas, and this voice type, like its soprano counterpart, is labeled as dramatic. A special kind of dramatic tenor, which we always associate with the operas of Richard Wagner, is the powerful German *Heldentenor*, or heroic tenor. Tristan is a Heldentenor.

Possibly the favorite among male voices is the baritone, the solo equivalent of the choral "first bass." Like mezzos, baritones have a range which lies between two other voices, bass and tenor. Though more often lyric, baritones may be dramatic as well.

Some authors expand this six-part listing by adding other "mezzo" voices: for example, mezzo-baritone or mezzo-tenor. Nevertheless, in order to keep within the scope of this book's program, you should learn only the division in Figure 4.1.

Building the Registration Technique

Despite the diversity of opinions on the nature and number of registers, almost all authorities agree that when building a registration technique, three disciplines are essential: (1) blending of the registers (so that any tone of the vocal gamut may be sung deliberately with any varying amoung of "weight" and with a minimum of strain); (2) exercising the *passaggio*, or bridge from one register to another; and (3) acquiring a facility in register adjustment, or, in bel canto terms, developing agility and flexibility.

Blending—and "mutation"—of the registers involves "weight" adjustment, in the sense of learning to bring the lighter adjustment into the heavy mechanism (or chest register) and vice versa, transferring the heavier adjustment into the lighter mechanism (head or falsetto register). Never attempt the latter technique without the supervision of a good teacher. You risk hoarseness, strain, nodules, and even paralysis if you do.

One of the first assignments in register development is the isolation and training of the area least used in the voice, the undeveloped register. As a general rule this area can be found in the upper register for men and the lower register for women.*

Having isolated the undeveloped register, you may begin to develop it with exercises that integrate developed parts of the voice with the undeveloped ones. For example, assuming that the male voice is less developed above middle C than below, apply this four-part exercise:

1. Starting on C above middle C, in falsetto, sing a two-octave descending scale on *mum*. Overdo the *m*, and check your breathing and posture.

2. Now repeat that exercise, but this time sing triplet *mum*s on each tone, or:

*I say "as a general rule" because of an experience I had teaching in a university in California. Having made this statement as an unqualified generalization, I was quite naturally surprised one year to discover that out of fifteen of my female students, *ten* had well-developed lower registers! Soon afterward I learned that these were drama majors with extensive stage experience and elocutionary practice.

mumumum - mumumum, etc.

3. Then repeat part 2 starting on B, then B♭, etc., until your final starting tone is F♯ above middle C.

4. Now reverse the starting-tone order of exercise 3, taking care to lighten up your voice around the midpoint, as you ascend.

For the ladies:

1. Do the same steps 1 and 2 as the gentlemen, in light adjustment, starting on G down to C above middle C as starting tones.

2. Next try this: Combine your breathing-attack skills with isolation of the chest register as you make a "deep sitting" attack on *huh*. Use the *h* to open the throat as you imagine a "buzzing" sensation in the chest area. Really "beef it up," that is, don't be afraid to get heavy in this register. Watch that the larynx ("Adam's apple") does *not* rise appreciably. With this exercise you will have planted the seed which will blossom into the technique of "chesting," or utilizing maximum chest voice.

3. Now repeat the first exercise, but here attempt to "bring in" this chest voice as you descend. ("Chest" will normally come in around G or A.)

Blending and mutation of the registers also requires the ability to make adjustments on an individual tone. For this purpose the bel canto school offers its most sophisticated vocalise, the *messa di voce*. While the *messa di voce* (It. "placing of the voice") is primarily a device for swelling the tone, it has several secondary functions such as developing vocal power and "ring" (Chapter 6), blending of the registers, and "placement" adjustment (Chapter 6). Do not practice the messa di voce without supervision.

Here is how it works. Take one tone (middle C for bass, E♭ above C for tenor, A♭ above C for alto, D♭ above octave C for soprano) and phonate on *Kah:*

1. In the lightest adjustment possible.

2. Sustaining with energy.

3. Gradually increasing weight to a full, heavy adjustment.

4. Then reverse.

It is in the midst of the reverse process that you will suddenly become aware of the importance of good breath management in executing the messa di voce.

The vocalise is musically graphed in Example 4.1.

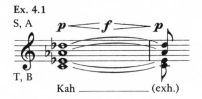

Ex. 4.1

Continue down the scale by half steps until the final starting note B/E♭/B/A♭ (S–A–T–B).

The *passaggio* (It. "passage") is the bridging area between registers located approximately between middle C and F♯. A replicate passaggio, called by some authorities the "secondary passaggio," is located in the female voice approximately one octave above the primary passaggio.

In terms of registration we can narrow the problem of passaggio development to one of adjustment facility. For male voices, the passaggio is the transition area where the singer must adjust from heavy to light mechanism (or chest to light/falsetto). Male singers with excellent training in registration achieve this bridging by mixing the two adjustments in the head register (hence the French phrase *voix mixte*).

Women must also mix adjustments somewhat in the primary passaggio. The real challenge for the female voice, nevertheless, is the use of adjustments in the head register in the secondary passaggio. Ignoring other factors for the moment, this mutation of registers is a matter of "flipping over" into a lighter texture.

Passaggio work involves both exercising register adjustments on tones within the passaggio area and practicing vocalises in which the voice must cross over from one register through the passagio to another.

An excellent example of the former is a series of messa di voce "workouts" on various tones found in the two passaggios. (The women may experience less resistance to the "flipping over" sensation if they try the secondary passaggio exercise on [o] instead of [a].)

There are several approaches to the crossover, all of which point back to one serious premise in registration training: Never "shove up" to a higher tone, but become accustomed to adding weight gradually until, with ample practice, the heavy adjustment can be used freely in the upper register without fear of damage to the voice.

Another principle is what I have called the "penultimate note principle." This simply means that the way the note directly preceding the high note is sung will determine the success or failure of the execution of the high note. The registration exercises in Examples 4.2 and 4.3 exemplify this principle.*

Ex. 4.2
For men (Notice the adjustments at "X")

Ex. 4.3
For women (Notice the adjustments at "X")

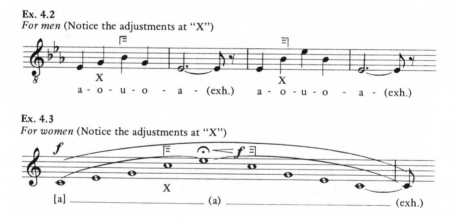

In both instances strive for a correspondence in adjustments between the note in the ascending pattern (marked ⊩) and the same note in the descending pattern (marked ⊣). It is a psychological obstacle, and not a technical deficiency, that causes us to think we must sing the two differently.

---

*Examples 4.2, 4.3, and 4.4 are exercises adapted from Burton Garlinghouse's unpublished "Vocalizing Patterns," pp. 1–2.

Another practice in registration adjustments—and a fore-taste of resonation drill—is the exercise in Example 4.4, for all voices. As you sing this adjustment practice, give a nice "buzzy" *m* on the attacks and pay attention to the notes marked "X" and ⊫, ⊒ , seeking always to maintain space and freedom.*

Ex. 4.4

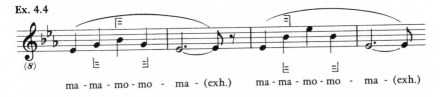

ma - ma - mo - mo - ma - (exh.)   ma - ma - mo - mo - ma - (exh.)

The third factor in register discipline is the bel canto study of agility and flexibility. "Agility," in the words of Garcia (*Treatise*, p. 10), is "the ability to conduct the voice from one note to another through all intermediate sounds." You have already made some progress toward perfect agility, with your work on adjustments and the passaggio. In fact, you may complete your study of agility by simply reviewing the two basic techniques of *legato* and *marcato* (a percussive attack—our *huh*). Then you may turn to the study of flexibility and its germinal skill, the *staccato*.

Flexibility—or elasticity, or plasticity—is the facility of moving from one volume of tone to another, easily. Its exponent, the staccato line, should be conceived as a rapid succession of tiny inhale–exhale, attack–release patterns. Another image that describes staccato is a series of notes separated by spaces. At all events remember that although staccato singing is detached, it is still a line: the notes and rests—attacks and releases—all fit into the time sequence of the line.

Review the "panting dog" exercise introduced at the end of Chapter 2. Do you notice that during this practice the belly (technically the epigastrium) bounces? Memorize this sensation; it forms the foundation for staccato attack and release.

A good starting point for staccato drill is an eight-note staccato iteration (repetition) on the primary vowels (see Example 4.5).

*These exercises are adapted from Burton Garlinghouse's unpublished "Vocalizing Patterns," pp. 1–2.

Ex. 4.5
S, A

T, B

1. [a] _____ (inh.)
2. [e] _____ (inh.)
3. [i] _____ (inh.)
4. [o] _____ (inh.)
5. [u] _____ (inh.)

Now, standing before a mirror (full length, if possible), judge yourself fairly on the exercise in Example 4.6, which you will first sing staccato, then legato. Your critique centers on (1) posture and breathing; (2) facility in adjustments (especially light at the top, heavy at the bottom); and (3) flexibility (including pitch accuracy and freedom).

Ex. 4.6

(8) [h]a _____ (exh.)

As you practice the more advanced exercise in Example 4.7, which combines both adjustment and flexibility training, try not to lose your concentration on the "X" and ⊨, ≡⏋ notes, even though your attention is focused on the staccato drill.

Ex. 4.7

(8) [a]___ [e] ⊨___ X [a] ___ ≡⏋[e] ___ [a]__ (exh.)

At this stage the paramount importance of a solid breathing technique to a proper facility of registration adjustment should be self-evident. Not one facet of the registration discipline is left untouched by a faulty breathing technique—not adjustment agility, blending of registers, swelling of the voice, or flexibility. If for any of these skills your proficiency seems to be developing unusually slowly, investigate your breathing technique.

Our final registration exercise (Example 4.8) is comprehensive. Use it to review all your knowledge of breathing and registration techniques, and focus your attention on the quarter rest in measure 2. How you breathe and adjust will determine how you make that upper register attack on the A.*

Ex. 4.8

Now you know the "basics" of registration. In singing, registration, like breathing, only "means" something in relation to tone, i.e., vowels. That relationship is the subject of the following chapter.

Study Questions and Exercises

1. Why is the "one register" approach the ideal for all teachers, in terms of the registration facility presented in this chapter?

2. Distinguish between adjustment and register.

3. Vennard (1967, p. 76) warns that "it does no harm for a man to develop his falsetto downward, but forcing the female chest voice upward is dangerous if not actually malpractice." What does he mean, and why is he so emphatic? Unfortunately, the latter practice does take place in studios all over the world. Why is that unfortunate—what is the injury? What do you suggest is the correct treatment of the upper register in the female (and for that matter, male) voice?

4. Practice the following exercise, which consists of an original motive (O); the motive backward, or retrograde (R); and a variation (V). Be sure the R and V phrases are attacked with a light adjustment. Take care how you breathe on the rests, and do not overlook ⊨, ⊣ and "X" notes (line 1).*

*Adapted from Garlinghouse, p. 2.

Repeat, using the vowels on line 2.

5. Look for "X" note adjustments (and ⊨, ⊣), and watch your breathing on rests, as you practice this one.*

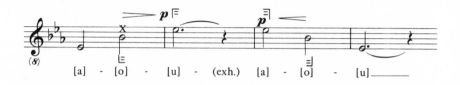

              [a] - [o] - [u] - (exh.) [a] - [o] - [u]____

6. Now review Sieber no. 1. Mark all "penultimate note" adjustments (X) and all "same note" (⊨, ⊣) adjustments; circle rests between phrases (especially the salient quarter rests). Practice the entire Sieber no. 1 legato, on vowels only. Now sing the entire first exercise, paying attention to all facets of posture, breathing, and registration. Now do exactly the same for Sieber no. 2.

7. Once more on Sieber no. 1: mark all sustained notes at the ends of phrases with messa di voce $p < f > p$ indications (for example, at *po* and *ni* in the soprano book). Isolate and practice these messa di voce tones. Repeat for Sieber no. 2 (*ni, da,* and *tu* for soprano). Now sing both exercises as a summary study for Chapters 2, 3, and 4.

*Adapted from Garlinghouse, p. 2.

Chapter 5

Registration and Vowels

Let the singer lighten the tone, even in the lower register, as he ascends the scale, and by the same reasoning, let him "fill out" the upper register, as he descends the scale.

—Weldon Whitlock,
*Bel Canto for the
Twentieth Century*

LET US REVIEW the five primary vowels, ranking them in psychological-imagery terms from "brighter" to "darker," with [a] as the midpoint (see Figure 5.1).

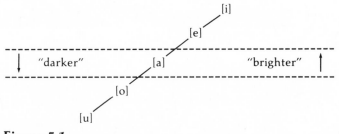

Figure 5.1.

Sing two progressions sostenuto on one comfortable pitch: first, the brighter series, [a]–[e]–[i], followed by the darker group, [a]–[o]–[u]. If you compare these two successions as

33

sensations, you will begin to notice that the brighter vowels feel rather "forward," in the masque area (i.e., around the cheek-bones, the nose bridge, and the eyes). The darker vowels you sense farther "back" in the mouth. Hold onto that observation; we will return to this description in the next chapter. For now, let us turn our attention to the connection between vowels and registration, or more specifically, vowel modification.

Vowels sometimes must be colored with the "round vowels" [o] and [u] to create "space" for certain tones in a register or passaggio. Such an adjustment of vowels to accommodate registration problems is known as vowel modification.*

One such need for vowel modification immediately comes to mind: the problem of vowels in the secondary passaggio, obviously a concern for women's voices. While the female voice can sing [o] and [u] rather comfortably in the primary passaggio, it is virtually impossible for it to produce a pure [u] above octave C. Sing [u] on an octave F#, ladies, and what you will discover is that your [u] is modified—in reality you are singing [o]! The [a] also will need to be modified in this part of the female voice, with the throat adjusting to an [o] shape to avoid "pinching." To accommodate both registration and resonation demands the forward vowels [e] and [i] are modified in both passaggios. As you sing [e] and [i] in the lower register, try to avoid "shallowness" by bringing in the [u] throat, so that

[e] = [u] throat + [e] masque (forward vowel),
and   [i] = [u] throat + [i] masque (forward vowel).

Now practice the two exercises for female voices shown in Example 5.1, remembering to form the vowel before breathing and to watch the breath on the quarter-note rest.

Ex. 5.1

| | (1) [u] | - | [o] | - | [e] | - | (exh.) | [u] | - | [e] | - | (exh.) and |
| | (2) [u] | - | [o] | - | [i] | - | (exh.) | [u] | - | [i] | - | (exh.) |

As you sing [e] and [i] in the upper register, you may avoid pinching by bringing in the [a] (or [o] if you prefer) throat, so that

*Vowel modification as a problem in resonation is the subject of Chapter 7.

> [e] = [a] (or [o]) throat + [e] "top,"
> and [i] = [a] (or [o]) throat + [i] "top."

Now practice in the secondary passaggio, sustaining but not forced, the exercises shown in Example 5.2.

Ex. 5.2

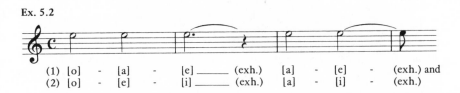

(1) [o] - [a] - [e] _____ (exh.) [a] - [e] - (exh.) and
(2) [o] - [e] - [i] _____ (exh.) [a] - [i] - (exh.)

For the men, the only potential vowel problem in the lower register is "muffling" the vowels, especially the back vowels [u] and [o]. This effect of bunching up the back of the tongue, often referred to as "swallowing the tone," can be avoided by using good posture technique, particularly with reference to the open throat and relaxed tongue. In the upper register treat the forward vowels [e] and [i] exactly as the women handle them in the primary passaggio. Review that description now, and then practice the two exercises for primary passaggio modification on middle C.

With modification on [a] in the male voice we come to a very important corollary to the rules of vowel modification, the concept of *covering*. While it applies to all vowels, "covering" has come to be used to describe the modification of [a] in the upper register of the male voice. In psychological-imagery terms, covering is a darkening of the vowel concomitant with a "flip-over" into the upper register. In mechanistic terms, covering is an expansion of the throat space together with a function change in the tongue and pharyngeal cavity (see Figure 6.1, next chapter).

To effect covering, maximize the throat space (as if yawning), modify the vowel slightly to a back vowel, and as you approach the "high note," think "down" as you sing "over." (If you can ever get hold of a recording by Pinza or Tozzi singing Verdi's *Di provenza il mar*, you will have a quintessential "aural image" of covering!)

Now practice the covering exercises in Example 5.3 for male voice in the tessitura of the passaggio. Where the vowel is indicated [a], sing a pure [a] or [ɑ]; cover for [a'].

Ex. 5.3

(1) [a] - [u] - [a'] - [a] (exh.); [a] - [a'] _____ [a] - (exh.) and
(2) [a] - [o] - [a'] - [a] (exh.); [a] - [a'] _____ [a] - (exh.)

In both instances think "down" as you sing "up."

The second corollary to vowel modification is the psychological-imagery notion of "focus." In common practice, when a listener describes a sung tone as being "fuzzy" or "spread" or "diffused," or another observes that it is "breathy," "swallowed," or lacks "ping" and "projection," these auditors are using psychological-imagery terms to describe a tone that is out of "focus." Continuing with this imagery, what this tone needs is clarity and "ring."

While "ring" is a matter for the following chapter, there is an aspect of "ring"—and a tool for creating it—which is germane to our study of registration and vowels. This is a focusing method known as *closing the vowel*.

The principle of closing the vowel derives from the "open–closed" dichotomy introduced in Chapter 3. In reviewing that discussion, you will recall that [ɛ] closes to [e]; [I] to [i]; [ʌ] to [o]; [U] to [u]. Closing the vowel simply means that when a vowel "spreads," as it is wont to do in the upper register, it can be "focused" by adjusting the sound to a more "closed vowel" color. In a like manner, an [a] that spreads can be focused with a slight modification to [o], and an out-of-focus [o] clarified by closing to [u].

Focusing and covering arose out of a need to preserve space and clarity in tones of the upper register. As the men may have already discovered, vowel spreading in the passaggio virtually "caps" the singer's range above middle C, creating a "roof" above the area of the "flip-over."

Then, too, the opposite effect is possible if focusing and covering are exaggerated. Every so often we hear a singer—frequently of the German school—who, in focusing or covering in the upper register, becomes too tight, too throaty. I admonish you, focusing the [e] and [i] should never involve a loss of throat space, for reasons that will become clear to you in the next chapter. If it does, you are either singing the wrong [e] and/or [i] or you have a posture and breathing flaw in your technique.

It is best to practice focusing and covering in conjunction with agility work. Slightly modify the base vowel as indicated, as you practice the scalar exercises in Examples 5.4 and 5.5. Make sure you do not close the throat as you close the vowel.

Ex. 5.4
For men

1.	[ɛ] _____ ([e]) _____ [ɛ] _____ (exh.)
2.	[I] _____ ([i]) _____ [I] _____ (exh.)
3.	[a] _____ ([a']) _____ [a] _____ (exh.)
4.	[a] _____ ([o]) _____ [a] _____ (exh.)
5.	[ʌ] _____ ([o]) _____ [ʌ] _____ (exh.)
6.	[o] _____ ([u]) _____ [o] _____ (exh.)

Ex. 5.5
For women

1.	[ɛ] _____ ([e]) _____ [ɛ] _____ (exh.)
2.	[I] _____ ([i]) _____ [I] _____ (exh.)
3.	[a] _____ ([o]) _____ [a] _____ (exh.)
4.	[ʌ] _____ ([o]) _____ [ʌ] _____ (exh.)

Now let us take a moment to reflect. At this juncture you have grasped two very important if complex concepts in vocal technique: (1) posture and breathing, and (2) registration. You have, as it were, a "model in your head" for your own singing skill. But note that the degree of perfection you attain in registration will determine the level to which you can rise in your work with resonation—just as your breathing proficiency affected your development in registration technique. Therefore, do not be in a rush to move on to the third function in artistic singing, resonation. Rather, be thorough with your practice in registration first, and be especially strict in the areas that overlap with resonation technique: vowel covering and closing. It will not take long for you to realize that as you were practicing the covering technique, you were forced to deal with a fundamental problem of balance between the forward and back vowels, between "ring" and throat space. This matter of balance is known as "placement," and it is the heart of the entire discussion in the next chapter.

Study Questions and Exercises*

1. "Covering" involves darkening the vowel; closing the vowel is often related to a forward sensation. Suppose a baritone wishes to sing an [a] toward [o], yet still keep the vowel forward and in focus. What is the balance problem here, and how would you have him achieve that balance?

2. If a soprano were to attempt to sing an [e] on a G in the secondary passaggio without any vowel modification, what would you expect to hear? A mezzo on F♯ in the same register on [i]? A soprano in the lower register on E♭ on [i] without a [u] throat? A tenor on A♭ above middle C on [i] without any [o] or [u] modification?

3. *Closing the vowels.* You are singing the vowel [ɛ] in the upper register and it is out of focus. To what vowel would you modify the [ɛ]? What about [ɑ]? [Y]? And finally, [œ]? (Review Chapter 3 if needed.)

4. *Review on register blending:* Practice these vocalises, paying careful attention to the ⌐, ¬ and "X" notes, focusing, and lighter adjustments on the "high notes":

1. [a] - [o] - [a] - [o] - [a] - [o] - [a] - (exh.)
2. [e] - [u] - [o] - [u] - [e] - [u] - [o] - (exh.)

5. Turn to Sieber nos. 3 and 4. Practice both exactly as you did for Study Question 6 of Chapter 4.

6. Practice Sieber nos. 3 and 4 exactly as you did for Study Question 7 of Chapter 4.

7. *Advanced agility exercise:* Practice the following, first slowly, then rapidly. Be attentive to vowel modification in the upper register.

[a] _____ (exh.)

*The more advanced student may wish to supplement these exercises with those found in Mathilde Marchesi's *Theoretical and Practical Vocal Method* (New York: Dover Publications, 1970).

Chapter 6

Resonation

The tone should resonate on the highest level consistent with the pitch, approaching the tone from above, not "sliding" or "pushing" up to the pitch before bending forward.

—Ralph M. Brown,
The Singing Voice

SIMPLY STATED, resonation is the production of resonance. Resonance is the result of the transmission of vibrations from one vibrating body (the *vibrator*) to another (the *resonator*). Think of resonance as a process of "sounding" (e.g., the struck strings of a piano) and of re-"sounding" or "resounding" (the sounding board of the piano).

What does resonance mean to a singer? To pursue that question further, you will need to know something about the vocal mechanism itself, and that discussion itself will require some agreement on some basic definitions. As you ponder these definitions, please refer to the model in Figure 6.1, a schematic cross-section:

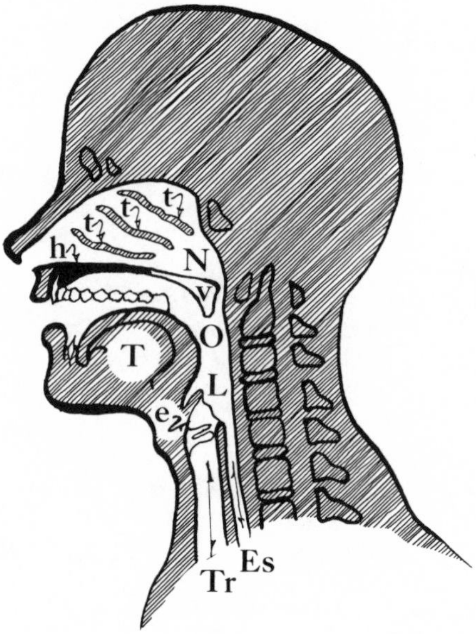

Es	ESOPHAGUS	e	EPIGLOTTIS
L	LARYNGO-	h	HARD PALATE
N	NASO-	t	TURBINATES
O	ORO-PHARYNX	v	VELUM
Tr	TRACHEA		
T	TONGUE		

Figure 6.1. Lateral view of the resonation mechanism.

Crystalize in your mind the locations of the *turbinates*, the *tongue* (noting where the tip is placed), the *hard palate*, the *soft palate* or *velum*, the *laryngo-pharynx*, the *oro-pharynx*, and the *epiglottis*. Every time you are confronted with a problem in resonation you will thank yourself that you have this mental model to fall back on.

As much as possible, try to create a mental image for each of the following terms:

1. *Resonance:* Reinforcement of sounds by synchronous vibrations.

2. *Fundamental, overtones:** "All the musical instruments produce composite sounds, consisting of the main sound or

*Definitions taken from Willi Apel, ed., *The Harvard Dictionary of Music* (Cambridge, Mass.: Harvard University Press, 1969).

fundamental plus a number of additional pure sounds, the so-called overtones, which, however, are not heard distinctly because their intensity (amplitude) is much less than that of the main sound. The frequencies of the overtones are exact multiples of the frequency of the fundamental."

3. *Partial:* Either a fundamental or its overtone in a series.

4. *Formant:* * In formant theory, characteristic partials of a tone lie within an absolutely fixed range of rather narrow limits, regardless of the higher or lower pitch of the fundamental. This characteristic "absolute range of partials" is called a formant.

5. *Formant theory:* The theory that the strong partial or partials of a tone will be determined by a fixed formant, and will be on the same frequency band, regardless of the pitch of the fundamental. This is largely true of vowel production.

6. *Forward brilliance:* Resonance "high in the head," sensation in the masque area; vis-à-vis "mellow" or "back" resonance.

7. *Projection:* Throwing or "carrying" the voice, similar to "forward brilliance."

Now to the question of how vocal resonation works. Turn back to Figure 6.1. Place a pencil on the diagram in such a way that the eraser end lies somewhere in the midst of the middle turbinate and the rest of the pencil is almost tangent to the back of the tongue (in the pharyngeal cavity). If that pencil were a seesaw and the fulcrum were located in the pharyngeal cavity, you could then imagine the problems of resonation as matters of balancing between the "large throat," or depth on the one end (the pointed tip of the pencil), and the "ping," "ring," or "forward brilliance" on the other end (the eraser end of the pencil). Now let us take a closer look at the two "ends" of the seesaw.

The term "large throat" comes from the classic dissertation on resonance by Wilmer T. Bartholomew. "The most effective

*Definitions taken from Willi Apel, ed., *The Harvard Dictionary of Music* (Cambridge, Mass.: Harvard University Press, 1969).

resonation," states Bartholomew, "is almost always found in that part of the back throat immediately above the larynx."*' Our main concern in resonation, as singers and teachers, is keeping this area free to vibrate by keeping the throat spacious. A spacious pharyngeal cavity, in other words, is a "large throat." In mechanistic terms, "large throat" means:

not swallowing — yawning!

1. A relative relaxing and lowering of the tongue, the back of the tongue, and the jaw (giving a sensation similar to "swallowing an apple").

2. An enlargement of the pharynx. There are three alternate ways of accomplishing this expansion:
   a. lowering the larynx.
   b. widening the sides of the throat.
   c. allowing the back of the tongue to move forward.

(Of the three methods, I find c. the least desirable, since it may inadvertently cause the larynx to rise.)

3. A comfortable lifting of the velum, provided:
   a. no undue muscular tension results.
   b. no entrance into the head passages is closed as a result of lifting of the soft palate.

Now let us put the concept of the large throat into practice. Stand in front of a mirror with your mouth poised as if to sing on [a]. Make yourself yawn several times. Notice how relaxed the throat and tongue feel. You should also become aware of the visibly increased throat space as the back of the tongue lowers, the walls of the throat widen, and the velum elevates. Immediately compare this posture with Figure 6.2, and make this another of your mental models.

Transfer that sensation now to an easy sostenuto *ah* ([ɑ] or [a]), and if you are singing with the large throat, you will discern that:

1. The larynx is low.

2. The pharyngeal cavity is "large."

*Wilmer T. Bartholomew, *Acoustics of Music* (New York: Prentice-Hall, 1945), pp. 139–159.

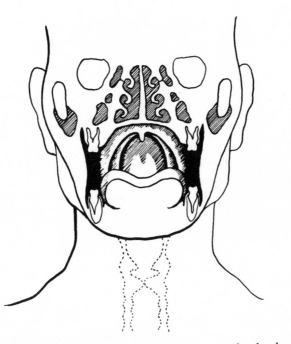

Figure 6.2. *Ah* posture. Notice the lowered tongue back, the widened walls of the throat, and the raised velum.

3. The tongue is relaxed and slightly furrowed.

4. The velum is arched.

5. The mouth cavity itself is spacious.

The vowels that are formed uniformly by rounding the lips and lowering the larynx obviously suit the large throat best. In terms of resonation, these back vowels [o], [u], and the covered [a'] favor the "pharyngeal end" of our seesaw. In acoustical terms these are referred to as the "low-formant vowels." (Until you have studied the next chapter, simply remember that "low-formant" means back vowels.)

Return to Figure 6.1 and the pencil imagery. If the tip of the pencil stands for the area of the large throat, the eraser end is that masque area which yields "forward brilliance" or "ping," or "ring." It is this ring that brings brilliance to the tone and the ideal in resonation which all singers seek for every tone in the voice. In mechanistic terms, ring is the presence of a strong, very high overtone characteristic of good or even loud vocal

tones, which is present in the tone regardless of the fundamental pitch, vowel sung, and even the voice type producing the
tone.

You may have already deduced for yourself that vis-à-vis the
low-formant vowels [o] and [u], the vowels most adaptable to
forward brilliance and ring are the forward vowels [e] and [i].
That is partially correct (pun intended), depending on which [e]
and [i] is being executed. For now it is important that you know
only how the forward vowels can be utilized to develop or
reinforce forward brilliance.

Imagine that a singer has a beautiful voice but a rather
lackluster tone quality. The brilliance and ping are wanting.
How can the individual "bring in" the ring?

There are three techniques for bringing ring into the masque
area, and hence three sets of gymnastics from which you can
select a method which develops ring most effectively in your
own instrument. They are: (1) exaggerate the high-formant
vowels; (2) practice various ng ([ŋ]) exercises; and/or (3) test
diverse vocal gymnastics on a hum, a buzz, or the "humming of
the tongue."

First, you can try exaggerating [e], [i], and even a very bright
ah. In the following exercise, you will "sing" several exclama-
tions having an initial m in the upper register. Be sure the m is
pure (and not ʌ-m) and that you do not shove. Now exclaim (in
falsetto for men, head voice for women):

1. Ma!

2. Me!

3. Mi!

The sound should be "twangy," "reedy," or even "piercing," but
at all events forward and quite focused. You might even sense a
little "tickle" around the nose bridge.

A second approach to reinforcing ring is also very effective—
if a little less raucous! This is a set of exercises based on the
velum-tongue sound of [ŋ], as in sing and song. Glancing at Figure
6.1, you notice that in forming the [ŋ], the passage from the
oro-pharynx to the naso-pharynx closes, "trapping" the tone in
the masque area.

It is crucial that in executing any of the [ŋ] exercises

1. The jaw is loose.

2. The vowel is formed first and maintained without jaw motion.

3. The neck is not stiff.

4. The "tongue-tilt" is perfected.

By "tongue-tilt" I mean simply that in going from any vowel to the [ŋ], only the back of the tongue moves, up and down. That is—and here I would refer to Figure 6.1—the tip of the tongue rests below the front teeth, and most important, the jaw must not move. Practice several sets of *ah-*[ŋ]*-ah* in front of a mirror to perfect the tongue-tilt before you attempt the [ŋ] drill.

Here is an elementary exercise in the [ŋ] approach. Standing before a large mirror, try out this three-step vocalise:

1. Form your large throat *ah* and repeat several *ah* attacks.

2. Try an *ah-*[ŋ]*-ah* sequence using the four points above as your critical checklist.

3. Now repeat (2), sustaining one comfortable tone on the *ah*'s.

Next, practice the more advanced resonance exercise in Example 6.1, using *ming-mong* to rhyme with *sing-song.** Sing the vowel very short and sustain [ŋ] with the jaw loose and the mouth "two fingers open." Begin to think already of carrying the ring into the vowel, and by all means do not scoop the *m*.

Ex. 6.1

(8) ming - mong - ming - (exh.)   ma - mo - ma - (exh.)

---

*All resonance exercises presented in this chapter are adapted from those found in either Burton Garlinghouse, "Vocalizing Patterns"—like this one— or Thomas Fillebrown, *Resonance in Singing and Speaking* (Philadelphia: Oliver Ditson Co., 1911), pp. 62–67.

Try that at several pitch levels, and then go on to the variation in Example 6.2 in the same manner.

Ex. 6.2

ming   mong   ming - (exh.)   mo - ma - mo - (exh.)

For want of a better term, I call the third approach to developing ring and forward brilliance the "buzz-hum" school. This school includes four interpretations. The first is a pure "buzz" itself. To perform a buzz, first flutter your lips in imitation of a horse. Add a spacious, sustained *ah* "behind " the flutter. As you do, you will notice—in psychological-imagery terms—three sensations:

1. The tone seems to "escape" from the nose as much as through the mouth.

2. The masque area "tickles."

3. A "cone of sound" seems to form from the masque area outward.

I often heard a variation of this exercise in the Akademie der Musik in Vienna which I termed the "buzz on the teeth." After fluttering the lips, say in rapid succession *ju-ji-ju-ji. . . .* This works well for some people, but it has the potential hazard of creating neck tension.

Another tactic is the hum. Humming is effective if executed correctly. A hum must always be accompanied by a large throat vowel, preferably *ah*. To develop ring by humming, form an *ah*, let an inner *h* make the attack, and maintain an open, yawn-like throat and mouth as you hum, sensing the tone "high in the head." The "triplet *mum*" exercise that is so useful in registration discipline is also an exponent of the *hum* approach.

The fourth derivative of the "buzz-hum" school is the invention of William Vennard; he called it the "humming of the tongue." It is not difficult to execute: Place the blade of the tongue between the upper and lower teeth and phonate on *ah* (you should then hear a sound akin to a buzzing *th* as in *without*). Complete this exercise by letting the "buzzing lisp" flow into the vowel (as in Example 6.3).

Ex. 6.3

(8)   t̆h _____ [a] ____ (exh.)

No matter which approach a teacher or singer applies—whether exaggerating the [e] and [i] vowels, working the [ŋ] into the vowel, or buzzing and humming—all are means to the same end: forward brilliance. One way may not be as efficacious for you as for someone else. Then try another "path" so long as it leads to the same "Rome."

And herein lies a crucial principle pertinent to all of the vocal disciplines and a caveat for the student and singer. No matter how bizarre an exercise may appear on first encounter, try it, but test it against this rule of "safety": So long as that exercise draws you closer to the vocal ideal you are seeking ("ring" or "mellowness," for example) and does a minimum of harm to other ideals in the process ("range" capacity, for example), pursue that direction. Otherwise, avoid it. I cannot exaggerate the importance of your using this rule to guide you and to protect you from the plight of vocal malpractice.

A key word in vocal training is *balance,* and the result of the perfect seesaw balance between the large throat and forward brilliance is known as *placement.* I deliberately say "result," for placement is not something a singer can "do" per se. Countless examples exist of attempts by singers to "place" this tone or that; to "place" this vowel higher or lower, back or forward. Never attempt to "place" a tone. In fact, avoid verbal forms of the word altogether: placement is an effect, not a cause.

The term "placement" obviously derives from the psychological-imagery school, in which it is used to describe the balance between "forward resonance and projection, approaching the tone from above," on the one hand, and "throat space," on the other. In bel canto terms, placement can be thought of as the result of pure vowels in harmonic balance with the "big tone." Mechanistically speaking, placement is the result of a balance between the ring or high-formant resonance and the reinforced low partial or low-formant resonance.

It is logical to assume that any maladjustments of that seesaw balance would result in faulty placement. That is exactly what happens, and the psychological-imagery school abounds in colorful terms to describe tones in whose production the balance is tipped "forward" and "back." Too "reedy" or "shallow," "metallic," "twangy," "smiley," "white," "hyper-nasal," "whiney," and "shrill"—all are commonly used to define tones that are "placed" too far "forward." To describe the opposite error, terms like "throaty," "hyponasal," "muddy," "swallowed," "gargled" (cf. Ger. *knödeled*), and "dull" are used. You might keep these terms in mind in case (heaven forbid) they are ever contained in a review of your technique.

In concluding this discussion, I would like to offer a general placement exercise which serves as a very expedient warm-up routine, as well. This is a *hung-ah* sequence on one sustained note, whose central purpose is bringing the ring into the vowel. Standing before a mirror, sing the following (Example 6.4) at various pitches:

Ex. 6.4

(8)   Hung ————— [a] —— (exh.)

Basically there are two stages to this vocalise: (1) all techniques leading up to the vowel, and (2) the passing of [ŋ] into the vowel. Before leaving (1), check that

1. The aggressive attack on the *h* is deep, and the larynx is low.

2. The vowel on [u] is pure and large throat.

3. The [ŋ] "buzzes," giving a heady feeling in the area of the turbinates.

4. All the rules of the tongue-tilt are observed.

5. The [a] as indicated in the exercise is formed in the throat before the back of the tongue is lowered.

Then carry the ring into the [a] as smoothly as possible. You may notice a slight *guh* sound at the transition point from [ŋ] to [a]. That is good; it indicates that you are executing the vocalise correctly.

Since resonation is undoubtedly the most intricate of the singing concepts, it might be well to recapitulate some major points from our analysis of resonation. If we could "plot" a course for the action of resonation, it would be in three stages (Vennard, 1967, p. 81):

1. The vocal lips produce a tone with a desired pitch, considerable volume, and complex timbre.

2. As this tone passes through the throat and the mouth, these cavities encourage those partials which make for power and beauty, and muffle the undesirable ones.

3. The final step is maintenance of balance among these partials, a process which results in proper placement.

We can now determine that a voice is healthy and resonant when it exhibits these three characteristics (Bartholomew, 1945, p. 141). Such a voice will have:

1. Vibrato, life, or warmth.

2. Low-formant resonance—roundness of sound.

3. High-formant ring—shimmer in the tone.

Also, in light of our original contention that singing is a synthesis of habits, we should observe resonation in relation to breathing and to registration. By including breathing requirements, we now have a set of six "vital signs" to good resonance (de Young, 1958, p. 62):

1. Accurate, sustained pitch, focused through tone and imagination.

2. Clear vowel quality based on formant reinforcement.

3. Tone level established from [ŋ] (and other) sources.

4. Clear and diaphragmatic attack.

5. Sostenuto breath control.

6. "Sensed" rather than "felt" awareness of projection of tone.

When we come to realize that resonation is a result not only of purity of vowel quality but also of conscious and correct registration technique, one age-old problem in projection becomes abundantly clear to teacher and singer alike: "weight" versus "placement." In short, I mean the common practice of projecting by "getting heavier" rather than "adding brilliance."

Remember Bartholomew's description (p. 148): ring is present in good (well placed) or loud tones. That means singers can increase their projection by getting heavy (adding weight and getting loud) or by adjusting the forward–back balance to achieve good placement—or both. Obviously the solution of adjusting placement is infinitely preferable to the more strenuous and potentially damaging prospect of adding weight. Yet how many times have you been subjected to the monochromatic "bellowing baritone" or the equally unpleasant warble of an abused soprano instrument? The next time some listener reports "I can't hear you," consider if your solution lies in adjusting your technique in registration, or resonation.

You have viewed vowels in relation to breathing and to registration. Now, with your knowledge of formants and placement securely tucked under your belt, you are poised and ready for the most sophisticated concept of tone in singing, the relation of vowels and resonation.

Study Questions and Exercises

1. What is the overtone series? What are harmonics? Partials? A fundamental? A formant?

2. Why is it that inexperienced singers so often "shove up" to notes in the upper register? What should they do instead? Would work on the messa di voce help? How (or why not)? Would a discussion of resonation help? How (or why not)?

3. What are the three methods for developing ring in the voice? Try all of the suggested exercises. Which work(s) best for you? Why?

4. Practice Sieber no. 5 completely through on one vowel, four times, in this order: [o], [u], [e], and [i]. Did you notice any loss of ring on [u] or [o]? Where? Any "throatiness"? How did you compensate for these flaws in resonation?

5. Repeat Study Question 4 for Sieber nos. 6, 7, and 8.

6. On Sieber nos. 5–8 did you notice any notes in the upper register which would be suitable for a swell (e.g., soprano no. 5 at *be* on F♯)? Practice a messa di voce on each of these. What did you notice about the ring in the swell? What about projection?

7. Practice these resonation exercises (based on Fillebrown, pp. 62ff):

a.

(1) Hung ——— [i] ————————————————— (exh.)
(2) Hung ——— [u] ————————————————— (exh.)
(3) Hung ——— [o] ————————————————— (exh.)
(4) Hung ——— [a] ————————————————— (exh.)

b.

(Hung - [i] - [u] - [o] - [a]——— (exh.)

c.

(1) Hung——— [i]————————— (exh.)
(2) Hung——— [u]————————— (exh.)
(3) Hung——— [o]————————— (exh.)
(4) Hung ——— [a]————————— (exh.)

Chapter 7

Resonation
and Vowels

*[The vocal cords] are responsible through resonance for the overtones
which determine the various vowels and types of voice quality . . . the
vowels themselves are produced by changes in the shape of the organs
above this lower back [throat] resonator.*

—Wilmer T. Bartholomew,
Acoustics of Music

IN TREATING the subject of resonance and vowels,
we will once again need to set forth some terms on whose
meanings we must agree—some new terms and also some
familiar terms with new meanings:

1. *Formant:* cavity or cavities in the resonance system that
   tend to produce a particular frequency among the
   overtones.

2. *Sympathetic vibration:* exciting a second vibrator having no
   connection with the first except the air (cf. resonance).

3. *Epiglottis:* leaf-shaped cartilage forming a lid for the larynx.

4. *Low-formant* vowels: vowels having relatively low second
   formants.

5. *High-formant* vowels: vowels having relatively high second
   formants.

We have analyzed vowel production as a function in breathing and registration. In this chapter we will determine what the process of forming and producing a vowel sound means, in mechanistic terms. For in reality, that process is the heart of vocal resonation itself.

A vowel is formed by the leaning over backward of the epiglottis over the larynx (see Figure 6.1). The changing of the position of the epiglottis forms different-shaped cavities, this giving a combination of resonances at different pitches. It is the unconscious adjustment of these cavities that forms the different vowels.

This adjustment is, I hasten to add, influenced by the change in the shape of the throat and tongue. Pure vowels, then, are the final consummation of this adjustment in its most accurate state.

Let us review the primary vowels, again, only this time in the following order (sing, in front of a mirror): [u]–[o]–[a]–[e]–[i]. For your edification, that order proceeds from lowest low-formant to highest high-formant vowels.

An aid in vowel conception is the vowel triangle. In the following discussion we will develop our own rather inclusive vowel triangle and then apply it to our notion of placement. We will then close the chapter with an analysis of vowels and color, or timbre.

Using [a] as the apex, we may construct a triangle of vowels. Later on, as you develop an awareness of the dynamic interrelationship of vowels, you will want to conceive of the triangle more in three-dimensional terms, as a cone with [a] as its axis. For now, study the rudimentary triangle in Figure 7.1. You may question why we are using [a] as the apex. Of all the vowels [a] is probably the nearest to the original glottal sound, which means it makes the least demands for modification of the sound produced by the vocal cords. It is also the loudest sound, and the most efficient.

Now roll up your sleeves, and let's really "dig in" to vowel formants. In the triangle, the vowels in the lower half—[a], [o], [u]—are single-formant vowels. Those above—[e] and [i]—are double-formant vowels. That means simply that the former have only one characteristic partial—the formant—while the latter have two different formants.

That defines single- and double-formant vowels; now let me

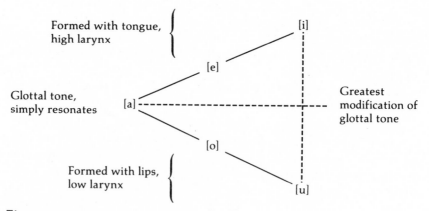

Figure 7.1

help you conceive them. You will notice in Figure 7.2 a scheme devised by William Vennard (1967, p. 127) to classify various findings on formant research. It is the clearest explanation I have ever found for single- and double-formant theory, and so I am happy to present it here. The vertical strokes symbolize formants recorded by different scientists of different singers singing the five primary vowels. The fact that the findings for each vowel are not exactly at the same pitch level is insignificant. What is important for us is the cogent exposure of high and low formants.

Notice the keyboard at the base of the diagram. As you can see, the [u] formant lies somewhere around middle C, the [o] around B♭ above, the [a] around high C, and so forth. Notice that [e] and [i] have two formant "clusters," a lower and an upper.

The practical implications of these double-formant discoveries are now clear: With the [e] and [i] you have a choice of singing either the shallow single-formant vowel or bringing in the large throat and singing the double-formant vowel. The latter is preferred. And while you are exploring this avenue of thought, imagine the implications of single- and double-formants for covering and focusing.

Let us continue to expand the vowel triangle, as shown in Figure 7.3, by including single- and double-formant vowels (letting [e'] and [i'] stand for the double-formant vowels). Read the triangle like a map: the further "south" you travel with [e] and [i], the more characteristically low-formant you become. That is to say, the implication from this diagram—that a

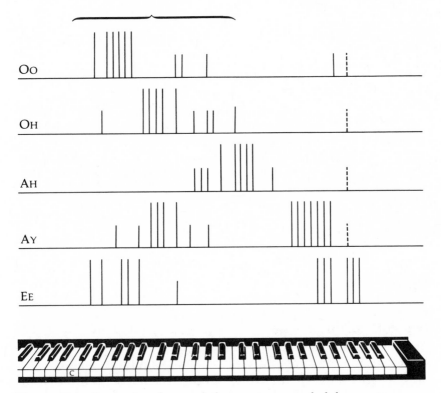

Figure 7.2. Synopsis of vowel formants recorded by various researchers (Vennard, 1967, p. 127). Copyright © 1968 by Carl Fischer, Inc., New York. Used by permission of Carl Fischer, Inc., New York.

difference between [e'] and [i'] and [e] and [i] is that in the former the larynx is lowered and the lips function to form the sound—is correct. Practically there is also an implication that if your [i] is too shrill, for example, sing a more rounded [i'], effectively rounding the lips and lowering the larynx. This is precisely what you do when executing the German technique of "umlauting," or turning [e] into [ö]! Just remember, the further "south" you move on the vowel triangle, the further back are the vowel sounds produced, and vice versa.*

The recognition of vowel resonance adds a new dimension to

*In point of fact German phoneticists utilize a triangle not unlike our vowel triangle. Tilt the triangle in Figure 7.3 45 degrees counterclockwise until [a] is the base of an inverted pyramid. If you can imagine the [u] as the oropharynx and the [i] as the front teeth, you will have in your mind a placement image used by phoneticists.

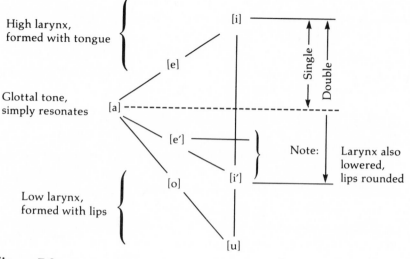

Figure 7.3

our concept of the seesaw balance in placement. Now, for instance, if we wish to make an adjustment from forward to back, we may regard that adjustment simply as a shift from single- to double-formant [e] and [i]. And Vennard's well-known summary takes on a whole new meaning for singer and teacher (1967, p. 145):

> The brilliant vowels, [e] and [i], should not offer too much problem when we remember that they are actually [o] and [u] with added high formants. The chief difference between them and the vowel [ɑ] is in the proportions of their overtones. In [ɑ] "ring" and mellowness are equally balanced, while in [i] the "ring" is higher pitched and may overpower the lower partial. This is what happens when the [i] sounds strident, "white" or nasal. In such a case the [u] which is underlying the [i] sound is being muffled by a tongue that arches too high, or is being obscured by a forward resonator that is too strongly activated. . . .

And now let us take up resonance and vowel color, or *timbre*. Review the vowel chart at the end of Chapter 3, and then compare that chart with our fully developed vowel triangle. In terms of vowel color, moving "south" on our triangle implies darkening the vowel; moving "north" lightens it. This light–dark modification, called in Italian *chiaroscuro*, is the most fundamental color or timbre variation.

Superimpose the vowel chart on the vowel triangle.

Remember that to darken the vowel you need to move "south" on the triangle. Given the superimposition, then, it follows that you may darken [i] to [i'] or beyond, for example, to the French [y], and so on. Theoretically, to darken [e] we travel "south" through [e'] conceivably as far as [œ], the darkest extreme of [o]. An [a] may approximate to [o] as [ɒ] and [ɔ]. If you were to carry this synthesis to its logical conclusion, you would derive a very thorough version of vowel approximation along the lines of Garcia's *Hints on Singing* (p. 12).

Such an exercise is useful in building a frame of reference for the myriad possible colors at our disposal. Vowel coloring takes on its fullest meaning, nevertheless, when it goes beyond *tone* into the realm of *characterization*. Although vowel coloring for this purpose is the subject of Chapter 13, you might enjoy a preliminary glimpse of the relationship between chiaroscuro and characterization. Amuse yourself with the following set of vowel comparisons, a virtually involuntary modification:

Compare the [a] of *calm* with that of *sot!* Or the

[e] in *Weh* (Ger. "woe") with that of *Ehe* (Ger. "marriage").

[i] in *serene* with that of the adjective *mean.*

[o] in *holy* with that of *hotel.*

[u] in *doux* (Fr. "sweet") with that of *mourir* (Fr. "to die").

Garcia advocated repetitions on all shades of the primary vowels. There are two means for carrying out this exercise. One is to review the chart at the end of Chapter 3 by chanting each vowel cluster in any order but as a conscious modification of the primary vowels. In such a way, for instance, you recognize that [ɔ] is a variation of [a].

Alternatively, you may refer to Fillebrown's *Resonance in Singing and Speaking* (1911). In that event you may wish to practice selected examples like the following (speak through once, then sing the entire sequence sostenuto):*

ni nI nɛ ne nɔ nɑ nigh na no nə nɛ nʌ no nU nu
(1)   (8)   (1')

---

*Adapted from p. 20. As an additional option, sing each syllable on scale steps indicated by the arabic numerals. Also, the more advanced student might wish to sing a messa di voce with the progression 1–8–1'.

You have now completed the third—and most comprehensive—stage in your technical development. Hand in hand with setting the foundation for lessons in diction and interpretation, you have learned all that this study can offer you about the fundamentals of tone production. We now move on to the final lesson in technical development, articulation. In short, it is time now to set aside our work on vowels and concentrate on the way we use lips, tongue, teeth, and throat to project consonants.

Study Questions and Exercises

1. Edit Sieber nos. 9–12 with personal reminders regarding posture and breathing, registration, and resonation and vowels. Do not fail to take advantage of any opportunities to practice messa di voce phrases. Above all, scrutinize your breathing technique: it is the foundation of your vocal craft.

2. *Double formants:*

Sing:

[i] - [i'] _____ [i] - (exh.)

   at various pitches in the passaggio. Avoid any jaw motion on the leaps and any disruption of the placement balance. Repeat for [e]–[e']–[e].

3. *Timbre:* Make a list of all the vowels and their variations from brightest to darkest (and if you become hopelessly frustrated, see Vennard, 1967, p. 136). Then, for fun, give a poetic, descriptive word arbitrarily to each symbol (say, "chocolate" for [ɔ]). Now sing sostenuto your entire series, observing both technique and imagery for each tone color.

4. Repeat the "ni-nI, etc." exercise, substituting *p*, then *b*, and finally *m* for the nasal *n* attack. Do you notice any difference in resonation between the *p* and the *n*? Why?

5. Repeat with *f; v; t; d;* and *th* attacks.

6. Once more with *ch, s, j,* and *k* attacks.

7. Many caricatures of "the voice teacher" show him or her eliciting "pear-shaped tones" and pure *ah*'s. In point of fact, this portrait is not all that far-fetched. What do you imagine by "pear-shaped tones"? In mechanistic and psychological-imagery terms, why is the discipline of "the pure *ah*" so fundamental to resonance and projection? To Space, Freedom, and Energy?

Chapter 8

Diction and Articulation

The consonants are produced by actually putting obstacles in the way of the free flow of the air stream, which deflect, hinder, or interrupt it. If the vowels can be considered the flesh of the sound body, the consonants are the bones that hold the flesh together.

—Kurt Adler, *Phonetics and Diction in Singing*

IN COMMON USAGE, unfortunately, the word "diction" has come to mean both enunciation and pronunciation. In an effort to prevent any ambiguity from creeping into my imagery, I am sometimes forced to be a bit arbitrary. "Diction" is no exception: For our purposes "diction" means pronunciation in the sense of "proper pronunciation"; "articulation" means enunciation in the sense of "articulate pronunciation." Now let us immediately proceed to the connection between posture and articulation, satisfying our original pledge to study singing as a synthesis of habits.

In most cases form the consonant after the vowel, giving the following order to initial posture:

1. Form the vowel in the throat, mouth (and lips where necessary).

2. Form the consonant.

3. Inhale through both vowels and consonants (exception: for consonants requiring the participation of the back of the tongue or throat, nose-breathing is preferable).

4. Attack from the abdomen, etc.

Executing consonant attacks in this order has an added advantage of minimizing any opportunity for mispronouncing *t*'s and *l*'s as guttural. Begin immediately, then, to respect consonants, like vowels, as "pure," consciously observing the correct use of the right mouth part for each consonant and consonant-cluster in articulation. And for all of us accustomed to American usage and all of its "barbarisms," this overriding word of warning: Never allow the throat to articulate consonants not calling for its participation, or to substitute for a consonant in a word such as *but*.

Garcia's arrangement of consonants according to oral function (lips, tongue, teeth, and throat) is the most succinct and practical, and easy to memorize. As you study each of the following groups, practice each consonant in front of a mirror so that you can clearly examine the functioning mouth parts.

The first group is the *labials*, so called because they utilize the lips:

p: say *puh*

b: say *buh* (and not *um-buh*)

m: say *mum* (maximize the nasality of *m* and do not say *um-mum*)

Next come those which combine lips and teeth, the *labiodentals:*

f: say *fah, off* (explosive,* complete closure of lips)

v: say *vah, love* (sustained,* partial closure; "buzz" the *v*)

---

*Garcia's dichotomy between "sustained" and "explosive" stands for the distinction between those consonants which "sound by vibrating the vocal cords" and those that are "nonvibrating." The same distinction is made in lyric diction (Chapters 9–12) as "voiced" versus "voiceless."

The third group is the *linguodentals,* those consonants employing the tongue-tip and teeth:

t (explosive): say *too* (not *uh-too*) and *but* (not *bu* + glottal stop)

d (mixed): say *do* (not *uhn-doo*) and *and* (not *æn* + glottal stop)

th (sustained): say *thee* (not *uhn-thee*) and *with* (not explosive *th*)

Those formed with the tongue and hard palate are called *linguopalatals:*

Pure explosive c (It. *c,* Ger. *ch*): say *cielo, mich*

Sustained linguopalatals:
l: say *eel* (not *ee-uhl*) and *la* (not *uh-la*)
n: say *noon* (forward, not *uh-noon*—exaggerate the nasality)
j: (Fr.): say *joi*
Soft ch (Fr., Ger.): say *enchanté, Schule*
Soft x (*ggs*): say *excelsis*
Soft s: say *rosy, was*
Soft z: say *zoo* (and not *uhn-zoo*)

Explosive linguopalatals:
Hard ch (Eng.): say *itch, chair*
Hard s (Ger., Eng.): say *sister, messy, Nussbaum*
r (mixed):
   a. Flipped: say *veddy-era*
   b. Rolled: say *terribile*

Finally, those consonants formed farthest "back" with the back of the tongue and throat (and sometimes soft palate) are known as *linguogutturals:*

Pure explosives (k family):
Hard c: say *factor*
k: say *strike, Kalmus*
ks or hard x: say *excite, mixture, duck's bill*

Mixed explosives:
Hard g: say *go* (not *un-go*)

Mixed sustained:
(Ger. *ch* and Sp. *j*): say *ach, Jorge*

Sustained pure:
  ng ([n̩]): say *singer* (not *sing-g*[ʒ]*r*)

Practice these "pure" consonants in front of a mirror, diligently and meticulously, examining your functioning lips, tongue, teeth, and throat as you do. Your elocution, I assure you, will take on a remarkable new "cleanness."

Keep in mind as you continue that "pure" consonants, like "pure" vowels, will have color variations. It will be to your advantage to solidify these five groups of consonants clearly in your mind before learning their variations. The point is a direct parallel to the comment at the end of Chapter 3: Never try a variation of a consonant such as *l*—an Italian *gl*, for example— until you have mastered the pure form of the linguopalatal *l*. You will also be at an advantage if, when you are called on to say a voiceless *w*, a word such as *whether* immediately comes to mind, and not *weather*.

With respect to our *cantus librātus* concept, our task in articulation does not end with learning to manage the oral technique alone. We have a two-leveled problem of balance here. On the first level, the clear, crisp enunciation of consonants (and semiconsonants) must never hamper good tone production. In this sense, remember: The function of the consonant is to interrupt the vowel without violating the good tone. For this reason I urge you to form the vowel first in the throat and mouth, then the consonant.

On a higher level there still remains a very subtle adjustment required to equalize articulation and the legato line. In this sense, remember: The function of the consonant is to interrupt the vowel slightly without perforating the line that connects vowels, that is, the legato line.

One remedy for this tone-articulation balance problem is the adoption of "tone syllables." This clever idea is especially useful in singing legato in English, with all of its explosive initial and final consonants. And the concept of ending each syllable with a vowel sound—the principle from which tone syllables derives— is universally regarded as the principle for legato singing.

The eminent choral pioneer and inventor of tone syllables, Fred Waring,* defined the procedure as follows:

Tone Syllables (Pennsylvania: Shawnee Press, 1945). See also by the same author, "Choral Singing Is Growing Up," *Educational Music Magazine* 23 (March 1944), pp. 9ff.

Emphasize those consonants having pitch ["sustained" or "voiced"] and pronounce those which have no pitch as though they were the initial sound of the following word.

In our usual manner, let us work on tone syllables in a song by marking a score according to a three-step plan:

Step 1. Underscore the sustained (voiced) consonants.

Step 2. Connect initial and final voiceless consonants with a slur line.

Step 3. The only exception in this linking process is a connection which would interfere with the poet's original meaning. Check for this exception and make corrections.

When you have completed these three simple steps your musical score should resemble the excerpt shown in Example 8.1 ("Sorrow Stay," a lute song by the Renaissance composer John Dowland [1563–1626], published in 1600 in his *Second Book of Songs or Airs*). Phonetically you would hear this except as b[ʌ]–td[ɑ]– un, etc., and later d[ɑ]– una – nd[ə]–r[ɑ]Iz, etc.

As is by now quite clear, I am sure, my approach includes more than the isolated singing technique itself. While it is quite an admirable accomplishment to be in control of every function of the lips, tongue, teeth, and throat, that facility in articulation is valueless if it overpowers your capacity in breathing, registration, and resonation. What beauty is lost, for example, if in the execution of a superb linguopalatal *g*, as in *God*, your technical limitations force the large throat to constrict?

As we turn now to the refinements and nuances of tone and articulation in four languages, some knowledge of which is required of every soloist, do not lose sight of the skill you have learned so far, nor fail to recall its niche in the whole of the art of singing.

Study Questions and Exercises

1. Take the five consonant groups and practice each group before a mirror. Remember to form the vowel first, then

Ex. 8.1

proceed to the consonant. Work from an *ah* throat as you speak and sing sostenuto.

2. What are some difficulties you encounter with final *t*'s and *d*'s? Initial and final *l*'s?

3. Practice the variations of *r*. (If you cannot roll the *r*, try repeating slowly "hʌ-rʌ," using a flipped *r*. Accelerate gradually until you are in rapid succession and the motion becomes virtually involuntary—that is a roll.) What is the "American *r*"? Why do so many dramatists and dialecticians have such disdain for it? As a singer, what do you find technically weak or harmful about this semiconsonant?

4. Select a group of hymns and/or folk songs for practice on "tone syllables." Check yourself that you are not phonating the neutral [ʌ] or [ə] between consonants. What is that sound you wish to avoid? What is wrong with it?

5. Practice articulation on Sieber nos. 13 and 14. Do this exercise by (a) whispering the entire vocalise; (b) singing on the vowels only; and (c) combining correct articulation (using the right mouth parts in the right manner) and legato in balance.

6. Repeat for Sieber nos. 15 and 16.

7. Review all of Sieber nos. 1–16 for all aspects of tone and articulation. Pick at random four to eight examples and practice them exactly as you did in the two previous study questions. Perform them in class.

Chapter 9

Summary of
Italian Diction

Perhaps more than any other language, Italian's continuity of vowels and possession of fewer consonants make it God's gift to the singing voice. . . . Correctly sung . . . it constitutes a continuum of sounds of ineffable beauty . . . of iridescent pearls dropping quietly into a shallow pool.

—Ralph Errolle, *Italian Diction for Singers*

THIS CHAPTER, as the title implies, is a cursory look at Italian diction with the purpose of exposing the singer to proper pronunciation in lyric diction and embellishing the work in tone and articulation. It is not the purpose of the diction summaries to be exhaustive, and the student eager to advance his or her knowledge of lyric diction can be assured that many excellent and thorough manuals exist.*

One principle is central to all foreign vowel sounds: Vowels are pure; they are not diphthonged unless specially indicated. The [ɑ] of *caro,* for instance, is not the American diphthong [aU], but the pure singular Italian *ah* [ɑ]. Remember that principle, and you will have achieved a lot toward understanding lyric diction in Italian.

*For example, see Evelina Colorni, *Singers' Italian: A Manual of Diction and Phonetics* (New York: Schirmer Books, 1970); and Errolle, *Italian Diction for Singers* (Boulder, Colorado: Pruett Press, 1963).

The format for Chapters 9–12 is the same: We shall study the vowels, then the consonants of each language, then certain rules indigenous to that language, and finally make some practical musical observations.

In Italian, the front vowels, [e], [ɛ], and [i], are those we have come to associate with "forward brilliance." The closed [e], as in *questo*, opens to [ɛ], as in *bene*. There is no open [i] in Italian, only the closed [i] as in *ridi*. In practicing the three front vowels, check to make sure you are not attaching a final [I] to the pure vowel.

Keeping the vowel pure and properly placed will be facilitated by maintaining proper posture in the body and the mouth itself. There are three characteristics of front-vowel formation you should remember:

1. The tip of the tongue remains in contact with the lower front teeth.

2. The front of the tongue slides forward and rises toward the hard palate.

3. Simultaneously with the tongue motion, the lips spread.

By contrast, the back vowels help to maintain "mellowness" and are the low-formant [o], [ɔ], and [u]. Avoid adding an ending [U] to the [o], and [ə] to the [u] and [ɔ]. In other words, keep the vowels pure.

The last vowel—there are only seven—is the Italian [ɑ], which is neither front nor back, but balanced between the two. The [ɑ] is brighter than the English [a] (which should tell you something about its placement). Examine your [ɑ] in front of a mirror. Is your tongue relaxed? Are your lips spread or rounded—they should not be.

And now the consonants. Remember this general rule for consonants in Italian: Single consonants are (1) short and (2) preceded by a long vowel. A sustained *amo* is not *amm-o*, then, but *a-a-a-mo*.

Logically the opposite is true for double consonants. Shorten the preceding vowel, thus creating time sufficient to lengthen the consonants. A sustained *quello* is thus *que-lllo* theoretically, but in any event, do *not* sing it *que-lo*.

We may examine the Italian consonants in much the same manner as we treated consonants in the general realm of articulation. The first group of consonants, named because they are pronounced with the tip of the tongue lightly touching the inside of the upper incisors, are the *dentals*. This group includes *l*, *n*, *d* (voiced), *t* (voiceless), and *r*. In all cases avoid the American *un* preparation (as in *un-dove*), and watch that the tip of your tongue either darts at the teeth (with *t*, *d*, and *n*) or brushes them in a flip (with *l*). You are already aware that the *r* may be flipped or rolled. Flip the *r*, generally, when it is a single consonant and between vowels. Roll the *r* when it is the first letter of a word (*ridi*), the final letter—generally (*cantar*)—or precedes or follows another consonant.

Now practice speaking the dentals with all seven pure vowels, first as single consonants, then as double. Then repeat, singing sostenuto, for tone-articulation balance.

From another angle, *t* combines with *p* and *k* to form the group known as *voiceless plosives*—"voiceless" because they are uttered without vibrating the vocal cords, and "plosives" because they require a complete stoppage of the flow of breath followed by a sudden explosive release of the breath. But do not aspirate, i.e., do not puff the breath as you release it. Executed correctly, *p* will approximate to *b*; *t* to *d*; and *k* to (hard) *g* (hint: compare mouth parts in each approximation). Besides the spelling *k*, you may come across the *k* sound in Italian as *c*, *ch*, *q*, *kk*, *cc*, *cch*, *cq*, or *qq*.

Now practice these plosives in front of a mirror, with attention to functioning mouth parts. Practice each with the seven vowels, spoken; then as double consonants, spoken; finally, sing both single and double sets sostenuto.

Contrary to *p*, *t*, and *k*, the voiced plosives *b*, *d*, and *g* must be totally voiced no matter if they are initial or final consonants, or are placed in between vowels. Practice the voiced plosives according to the same routine as the voiceless plosives. Keep examining your lips, tongue, teeth, and throat.

Both *s* and *z* may be voiced or voiceless. *S* is voiced (1) as a single consonant between vowels (*rosa*) and (2) as a consonant preceding a voiced consonant (*disgusto*). It is voiceless when it is (1) doubled (*stesso*), (2) initial (*soave*), (3) preceding a voiceless consonant (*desto*), and (4) following a consonant (*pensiero*).

Z, which when voiced is pronounced like *d* + *s* (Eng. "su*ds*"), and when voiceless is *t* + *s*, is, unfortunately for us, not terribly regular. It is voiced *and* voiceless in three positions: initial, medial, and double. And only the ear will condition you to pronounce *mezzo* voiced and *palazzo* voiceless! Practice *z* both ways, nevertheless.

Ambiguous also are *c, g,* and *Sc,* pronounced either as hard *c* (*k*) or soft *c* (*ch*). The former pronunciation (*k, g, sk*) happens when the consonants are followed by *a, o, u, l,* or *r.* Practice the hard pronunciation, then, on *caro, gara, scala, cura, scusare,* and *crudele.*

The latter pronunciation (like *ch,* like Eng. *hue,* and like *sch*) occurs when the consonants are followed by *e* or *i.* So practice *cello, cielo, getta, gioca, scena, and fascino.*

For doubling the same rules hold: hard preceding *o* or *a* (*piccolo, fuggo*); soft preceding *i* or *e* (*leggiere, uccello*).

But in Italian, the addition of *h* and *i* reverses these rules. *C, g,* and *sc,* when normally pronounced soft (as in *voce, amici, gentile, agitato, scena*), become hard with the insertion of h (as in *che, chiamo, ghetta, preghiera, scherzo, boschi*). *C, g,* and *sc,* normally pronounced hard (as in *contra, gusto, scusi*), are made soft by the addition of *i* (as in *cioccolata, ciao, giocoso, lascia, prosciutto*). Practice going from soft to hard until shifting becomes second nature.

Peculiar to Italian diction, additionally, is the pair of *prepalatal* consonants *gn* and *gli.* The former is close to the sound of our word *onion,* while the latter approximates the formation of our word *valiant.* The *gn,* as in *degno, montagna,* and *signore,* is executed with the tip of the tongue touching the lower teeth. The *gli,* as in *miglio, Gigli, famigli,* and *Pagliacci,* is performed as a single articulatory movement of the front—and not with the tip—of the tongue against the hard palate.

Finally, we come to the hybrid [j] and [w], neither consonants nor vowels. These are semiconsonants. Both are open and sustained, and tend to form a quasi-contraction with the vowel that succeeds them, usually *i* or *u,* respectively. Spelled with an *i* as in *fiora* and *aiuto,* the [j] shortens and combines producing the *y*-like fy[ɔ]ra, and ayut[ɔ] (not fi-[ɔ]r[a], [a]-i-ut[ɔ]). Likewise, the [w], which is spelled with a *u,* contracts so that *uomo* is closer to *womo* than *u-o-mo* (use the back of the tongue).

It is this use of semiconsonants in words of a single vowel that causes so much confusion for us non-Italians. Not only does the semiconsonant open the vowel of words like *puo* (p[wɔ]), but it changes the vowel from stressed to unstressed (i.e., pw[ɔ], not pu-[ɔ]). The confusion arises as to whether an ostensible monosyllable is a one-syllable semiconsonant (*piè*) or a two-syllable word (*pie*). I refer you to Colorni (pp. 110 ff.) for the lucid solution to this phonetic "Rubik's Cube"! While you are there, you may wish to glance at the section on diphthong and triphthong execution.

Now study the excerpt in Example 9.1 from the aria *Nina*.* Sing through these eleven bars on *lu*, noting the breath marks (X), and make note of these numbered references to the score:

1. Semiconsonant [j].

2. The *h* hardens, thus [ke].

3. [i], not [I], hence [in].

4. Double *t*, stopping the tone slightly.

5. Enjoy the long [ɑ]. Notice how much easier it is to negotiate this colorature on [ɑ] than on [a].

6. Double *F*, stopping the tone slightly.

7. *M* is not doubled, vowel is [i].

8. Soft *c*, no *h*, hence [tʃɛmbaⱡi].

9. *V* is voided, so *s* must be voiced, with vowel as [e].

10. Prepalatal *gl*; *ia* is a semiconsonant, thus [zve-ʎjɑ].

11. Again *ia* is a semiconsonant, thus [mjɑ].

Practice this excerpt until all points are clear, then present it in class.

Our brief survey, though limited, has not strayed from our purpose in this study: an introduction to Italian diction and an enrichment of tone-articulation comprehension. If a summary of Italian has done nothing more for your technique than this, it has already done a great deal: The pure vowels of Italian allow for no such "pollution" as unindicated diphthongs and glottal stops; and also, Italian, with its nonaspirating and fluid

*By Legrenzio V. Ciampi (1719–?). The whole aria can be found in *Twenty-Four Italian Songs and Arias*, ed. Theodore Baker (New York: G. Schirmer, 1948), pp. 72–73.

Ex. 9.1

Nina
Canzonetta

English version by
Dr. Theodore Baker

Attributed to
Giovanni Battista Pergolesi*
(1710-1736)

*Although this song was long attributed to Pergolesi, it was composed by Legrenzio Vincenzo Ciampi (1719 - ?)

consonants and pure vowels is the ideal language for the legato line.

French is also fluid, in a way, but more limited in range and dynamics. The arsis and thesis of the Tuscan legato is transformed in French into the noble Parisian *souplesse*.

Study Questions and Exercises

1. Stand before a mirror and practice the Italian [ɑ]. How does its formation visually differ from the [a]? Which is brighter? Which is more forward? Now practice [i], [e], and [ɛ]. Which is the most likely to lose focus? Try out [u], [o], and [ɔ]. Which of these three is the most difficult to focus?

2. Sing this pattern with several repetitions, *sostenuto*: [ɑ]–l[ɑ]–[ɑ]–m[ɑ]–[ɑ]–n[ɑ]–[ɑ]–t[ɑ]. Now follow with [ɑ] ll[ɑ]mm[ɑ]nn[ɑ]ttɑ. Sing both in alternation until you are clearly aware of the difference between single and double consonant articulation. Do not lose the sostenuto.

3. Why is it easier to sing legato in Italian than in English? Why are tone syllables unnecessary in Italian?

4. Study the Italian vowels carefully, then compare them with the material on vowels presented in Chapters 3, 5, and 7. What is "missing" in the Italian series? Italian is often characterized as a "bright" language. Explain this concept in light of your vowel research.

5. Practice Sieber nos. 17–20. Mark the vowels as Italian, and vary the syllable *be* as either [bɛ] or [be]. Do the same with [po] and [pɔ]. Apply messa di voce whenever possible. Practice consonants as Italian, keep working on legato, and reinforce your techniques of posture and breathing, registration, and resonation.

6. Take one short piece from the *Twenty-Four Italian Songs and Arias* (be sure the key—medium or low—suits your voice type). Go through this regime when learning a new piece: (a) Practice just the "notes" on *lu* in lighter adjustment, and repeat for breathing (paying close attention to the *rests* in between phrases); (b) practice the *text* separately, which you will have marked for diction according to this chapter; (c) practice both text and tone separately at tempo, then together *at a reduced tempo;* (d) repeat until close to memorized; and finally, (e) present in class.

7. Listen to several recordings of Italian arias and songs performed by artists such as Pinza, Tebaldi, Tozzi, Pavarotti, Gigli, Caruso, and others. Make some notes with respects to their breathing and registration, vowels and resonation, legato line, vocal chiaroscuro, and fine points of diction. Discuss and compare ideas in class.

Chapter 10

Summary of French Diction

But listen to the French! It sings, it floats, it pours, and it titillates the ear with its crisp, clean consonants, its pure, highly resonated frontal vowel sounds.

—Thomas Grubb,
*Singing in French**

Like the treatment of Italian in the previous chapter, this is a treatment of the salient points of diction in French. I highly recommend that you supplement this discussion with the excellent manuals by Richard G. Cox and Thomas Grubb.† For now, our concern is knowing the rules for vowel and consonant pronunciation in French, and the practical applications of those rules in singing.

As with Italian, vowels in French are for the most part pure; avoid the American diphthong. Moreover, in French, more than in any other language discussed in this study, it is extremely important that you differentiate between closed and open vowels.

*Copyright 1979 by Schirmer Books, a Division of Macmillan, Inc. Used by permission.
†Cox, *The Singer's Manual of German and French Diction* (New York: Schirmer Books, 1970). Grubb, *Singing in French* (New York: Schirmer Books, 1979).

Vowels in French can also be classified according to placement, as front or back. There are two kinds of front vowels: the strictly front [i], [e], [ɛ], and [a], and the rounded front [y], [ø], [œ], and [ə].

The [i] and [e] are quite similiar to their Italian equivalents. They are closed vowels. The [i] *sound* appears as the letters *i* (*ici*), *î* (*île*), *ie* (as a word ending), and *y* (*lys*). The [e] (and not [eI]) is spelled *ai* (in the final syllable), *é* (*été*), and frequently *e* before all final consonants (*pieds*).

The third front vowel, the open [ɛ], has many spellings: *è, ais, ai* (when not final), *aî, aie* in verb endings, *ei* (*peine*), and *es*. Its other spelling, *e*, can be distinguished from closed *e* when it is found: (1) before a pronounced final consonant, and generally, (2) before two or more consonants (*perdre*).

The final front vowel is [a], pronounced like the *ah* of the English *half*. It is spelled as either *a* (*car*) or *à* (*là*).

There are also four rounded front vowels. Don't let their appearance throw you; they are more familiar than you realize, when you remember:

1. [y] is pronounced with the throat in [a] position, lips rounded, giving it an [i] timbre. Think of [y] as a "closed *eu*." It is spelled generally as *u* (*une*), *û* (*dû*), *eu* (in parts of *avoir* only), and *ue* at the end of a word or syllable.

2. [ø] is [e] with lips rounded to [o]. It is spelled generally *eu* (*heureuse*) and *eû* (*jeûne*). Think of [ø] as an "open *eu*."

3. [œ] is [ɛ] with lips in [ɔ] position. [œ] is spelled generally *oe* (*oeil*), and exceptionally *eu* and *oeu* (*pleure, seule, peur, coeur*).

4. [ə] is the unstressed "schwa," pronounced midway between [ø] and [œ]. Most frequently the schwa is found as the final *e* or in third-person endings (*-aiment*) in sung French. The composer will indicate that he wishes the schwa to be sounded by giving the *e* a separate note (*image* in Fauré's *Après un Rêve*, for example).

In addition to the front vowels, there are four back vowels in French, the first three of which are pronounced by rounding the lips. These you know already as (1) [u], spelled generally *ou* (*toujours*) and *oû* (*goût*); (2) [o], spelled generally as *o* (*chose*), *ô* (*rôle*), and *eau* (*beau*); and (3) open [ɔ], also spelled *o* (*bonne*), and *au* before *r* (*aurore*). The fourth is the *ah* sound equivalent of the Italian [ɑ] and the English sound in *calm* and *father*. It is spelled generally *a* (*passer*) *â* (*grâce*) and *oi* (*bois*).

Now take a minute to review. Compare the twelve French vowels with the seven Italian equivalents, in front of a mirror.

Of paramount importance in the mastery of French diction is the learning of the four French nasals, [ɛ̃], [ɑ̃], [ɔ̃], and [œ̃]. These sounds, indigenous to the French language, occur when linked with an *n* or *m* that is final (*ton*) or precedes another consonant which is not *n* or *m* (*attendre*).

Practice only the four base vowels first, for throat and mouth placement. Then practice them as nasals along the lines of the following scheme, based on that of Pierre Bernac's *The Interpretation of French Song* (1972).

1. *in* [ɛ̃]   as in *Chopin*, like American *tan*
   (also im,
   sometimes *en*)

2. *en* [ɑ̃]   as in *encore*, like American *fawn*
   (also *an, am*   as in *chambre, chantant*)

3. *on* [ɔ̃]   as in *bon*, like English *tone*
   (also *om*   as in *sombre*)

4. *un* [œ̃]   as in *chacun*, like English *sun*
   (also *um*   as in *humble*)

Before we take up the French consonants, we need to examine the French *glides*, [j], [ɥ], and [w]. These glides are comparable to the semiconsonants in Italian. Like the Italian [j], the French [j] approximates to a [y] sound in English. It is spelled either *i* (as in *bien* = *b* + [j] + first nasal) and frequently *ll* (as in *fille*).

The [ɥ] also approximates to a [y] sound, but with the tongue in [i] position, not [u] position. It is spelled *u* (*lui, nuage*). The [w] corresponds to the Italian semiconsonant [w], but the lips are far more intensely rounded in French. It is spelled with an *o* before *i* (*joie, mois*) or *ou* before a vowel (*oui, jouer*).

Review the Italian semiconsonants and the French glides and compare how they sound and look.

We may simplify our classification of French consonants into three categories: (1) those which are pronounced like English equivalents; (2) those which are pronounced like Italian equivalents; and (3) those which are distinctively French.

Here are the consonants, with spellings, which are pronounced as in English:

1. [b]   as *b* (*arbre*) and *bb* (*abbé*)

2. [p]   as *p* (*plus*) and *pp* (*apporter*)

3. [g]   (hard) as *g* (*goût*) and *gg* before *a, o, u,* and a consonant (*aggrégat*)

4. [v]   as *v* (*vivre*)

5. [f]   as *f* (*faux*) and *ff, ph* (*effet, philosophie*)

6. [z]   as *s* (voiced) between two vowels (*rose*), *z* (*azur*), and *x* in liaison (*doux amis*)

7. [s]   as *s* (voiceless) (*sans*), *ss* (*laisser*), *ç* (*reçu*), and *t + i* (*nation*)

8. [ʒ]   as *j* generally (*je*), sometimes *g* (*mirage*)

9. [ʃ]   as *ch* (*toucher,* like English *sch*)

10. [m]   as *m* (*mer*), and *mm* (*comme*)

11. [n]   as *n* (*divine*), and *nn* (*Cannes*)

The division of consonants which are formed like the Italian equivalents is briefer (note, too, the difference in tongue positions from English equivalents):

1. [d]   as *d* (*odeur*) and *dd* (*addition*)

2. [t]   as *t* (*fête*), *tt* (*attendre*), and *the* (*théâtre*)

3. [k]   There are many spellings; the main spellings are *c* and *cc* before *a, o, u,* or consonant, and *c* final (*car, occuper, roc*)
q (*quel, co*)
k (rare: *kiosque*)

4. [ɲ]   as *gn* (*regner, digne*)

5. [r] as *r* (*cher, troubler*), and *rr* (*arriver, torrent*): note that it is flipped and forward.

To the third group belongs the French [l]. This sound is formed with the tip of the tongue behind the front teeth. It is spelled with *l* (*lointain*) and *ll* (*aller*). But note that the *ll* spelling only occasionally signifies the [l] sound—compare the [j] in *travaille* and *village*, for example.

The uniquely French use of *liaisons* can be confusing for foreigners unless we set down some rules for the application of these linking devices. A liaison occurs when a normally silent final consonant is pronounced before a word beginning with a vowel or a mute *h*.

There are nine occasions for the use of liaisons. I would not memorize the following checklist, but keep it as a reference. Use liaisons for a(n):

1. Article followed by an adjective or noun (*les hommes*).

2. Adjective followed by a noun (*mon ami*).

3. Numeral followed by an adjective or a noun (*deux amis*).

4. Adverb followed by an adjective or an adverb (*très utile*).

5. Personal pronoun (or *en*) followed by a verb (*nous arrivons*).

6. Verb followed by a personal pronoun (or *en*) (*prends en*).

7. Preposition followed by its complement (*en écoutant*).

8. *Quand* and its successive word (*quand il*).

9. Various forms of *avoir* and *être* and their successive words (*il est ici*).

I will pass on to you the best advice regarding liaisons that I have been given: Use them sparingly, and in any event, go over all your French pronunciation with a reliable diction coach.

And do not fail to realize that French, like Italian, is a language of *vowels*. Peculiar to French, thus, is the absence of audibly doubled consonants. Whereas the legato line is the ideal in Italian diction, the all-pervading rippling nature of the authentic Gallic line is the goal in French diction. It is a *souplesse*, a plastic, bubbling, unaccented expression, in which the singer strives to leave all syllables almost equally weighted.

No prototype better reflects these characteristics than the nocturnal seascape *Beau Soir** by Claude Debussy (1862–1918). Sing the excerpt in Example 10.1 through several times on the French vowel [ø], utilizing the "inhale" breathing style; avoid any accenting as you paint the beautiful *souplesse* lines.

Mark all the nasals as (1), (2), (3), and (4), as defined on p. 77. Isolate and practice the nasal words.

Circle each schwa.

Now focus your attention on the following references to the musical score:

    a. An *elision*, like the liaison, links *lorsque-au* (l[o]r–sk[o]).

    b. [o].

    c. [j] glide; avoid [ɛI] diphthong.

    d. pure [u].

    e. pure [o].

    f. pure [u].

    g. [y], not [u].

Next, monotonally and metronomically speak through the entire excerpt until the diction is flawless.

Sing completely through it on *one tone sostenuto* the same way as you spoke it.

Finally, sing it as written; repeat until fluent. Present it in class.

I am sometimes asked with which language I have the most difficulty in pronunciation. I usually respond that unquestionably French, because of its amazing subtlety, is the most elusive to learn to sing correctly, but not to sing. German, by contrast, is difficult for us foreigners to sing, because of the predominance of consonants and guttural articulation. As you will soon discover, it is no less beautiful for having that quality.

---

*In *56 Songs You Like To Sing* (New York: G. Schirmer, 1937), pp. 18 ff.

Ex. 10.1

Beau Soir
(Paul Bourget)

Evening Fair

English version by
Henry G. Chapman

Claude Debussy

87700

Study Questions and Exercises

1. Study and memorize the four French nasals until they become automatic in your sight-reading and intrinsic to your study plan. You will be delighted to discover what a timesaver this trick is.

2. Continue to practice your Sieber for vowel purity and articulation training. Study Sieber nos. 21–24 for technical work on tone and diction.

3. Why are the four "rounded" front vowels rounded? In other words, what is rounded? Compare this group with the other front vowels. How does rounding affect resonation? Projection? Focus?

4. Draw a connection between back vowels and the seesaw principle. Compare front vowels and back vowels with respect to placement. Do the same for the glides.

5. Compare several French songs and/or arias. What do you notice about the dynamic- and pitch (*tessitura*) ranges? Why is "inhale" breathing more appropriate to French art song? Describe the connection between legato and liaison. Would you say that French songs and arias are "cooler" or "warmer" than Italian?

6. Select one of those songs for presentation in class. Use exactly the same seven steps outlined above to prepare that presentation. Do not let your good techniques of breathing, registration, and resonation decline in the process of developing diction skills!

7. Listen to several recordings of French arias and mélodies (songs) performed by such artists as Pons, Simoneau, Bernac, Souzay, Singher, Baker, Teyte, Crespin, and others. Write down a critique on such elements as breathing, liaisons, and legato; resonance, vowels, and projection; range and registration; and nuances of diction. Discuss and compare ideas in class.

Chapter 11

Summary of
German Diction

The German mode of articulation . . . may be said to be characterized by the formation of vowels, especially the round vowels, and of the dentals . . . the tongue articulation being more forward and determined, and the lips freely used in the formation of vowel and consonant sounds. . . . To German ears, spoken English . . . sounds to a certain degree unarticulated.

—Wilhem Viëtor,
German Pronunciation

AFTER THE ADMITTEDLY strenuous exercise of the two previous chapters, this study of German diction* should come as a welcome relief. For there are no vowel sounds in German which you have not already encountered, and you will need to learn only a few new consonant sounds. Your main "antagonist" in singing in German is the so-called "Knödel, that bunching up in the laryngeal-pharynx area caused by an exaggeration of the umlaut. The umlaut (¨), whose ancestor was an inverted *e* placed so (ꝏ) over the vowel, is an addition to a pure vowel which rounds it toward the [e] sound. You will want to pay careful attention to your throat space, then, as you practice the diction exercises in vowels, diphthongs, and consonants.

*For a more in-depth examination of German diction, see Richard G. Cox, *The Singer's Manual of German and French Diction* (New York: Schirmer Books, 1970) and William Odom, *German for Singers* (New York: Schirmer Books, 1981).

83

TABLE 11.1

Closed	Open	Vowel Spelling
[i]	[I]	*i*
[e]	[ɛ]	*e*
[o]	[ɔ]	*o*
[u]	[U]	*u*
[y]	[Y]	*ü, y*
(Fr. *u*)		
[ɸ]	[œ]	*ö*
(Fr. *eu* closed)	(French *eu* open)	

The distinction between closed and open vowels is just as critical to German diction as it is to Italian and French. Review that dichotomy in Italian and French diction, then study the guide to German vowels in Table 11.1.

You know these vowels now according to their position as "front," "rounded front," and "back." Since that subdivision also holds true for the German vowels, we may now move on to the more specific region of the rules for opening and closing of the vowels.

In general, you will find open vowels in one of three positions:

1. Before two or more consonants, generally (*immer*).

2. In a monosyllable occasionally before a single final consonant (*ob*).

3. Before these sounds:
    a. *ch*—*i* and *e* always open (*ich*); *o* sometimes open (*doch*).
    b. *ck*—all vowels open (*Blicke*).
    c. *ng*—all vowels open (*singen*).
    d. *β* (pronounced as *ss*)—*i,e* always open (*essen*).
    e. *sch*—all vowels open (*Tisch*).

Closed vowels are more prevalent than open vowels in German. Broadly speaking, there are eight locations for closed vowels:

1. Before a single consonant followed by a vowel (*leben*).

2. Before *h* is the same syllable (*ihnen*).

3. As a doubled vowel (*Meer*).

4. In a final syllable (also, but note exceptions, notably the directional suffixes *her, hin, ob,* etc.).

5. Before a single final consonant in a monosyllable (*nun*) or in a stressed final (*Medizin*).

6. Before *ch* (generally: *suchen, hoch;* but cf. *doch* above).

7. Before *β* (sometimes: *grosse, süsse*).

8. Irregularly before two or more consonants (*Erde, schönste*).

Mark this list for ready reference; you will be needing it again in conjunction with Chapter 13.

The German [ə], which, like the French schwa, is a rounded front vowel, is prominent in the German language. The sound of the schwa, spelled generally *e,* occurs in unstressed syllables (as in our "*a*long," their "*ge*boren"), and particularly as the final, unstressed syllable (*Liebe*). Since the schwa is such an integral part of proper pronunciation in German, practice it again and again until it is perfected, avoiding the spread [æ], the flat [ʌ], and the unrounded [ɛ].

In sung German we encounter the same problem with diphthongs as with all languages: the proper execution of diphthongs on sustained notes. The rule is simply to sustain the primary vowel and, in such cases, close to the secondary vowel only at the last moment. If you wished to sustain *au* (*a* + *o*), for instance, you would hold out the [a], closing to the [o] just as you passed on to the next tone.

In German lyric diction there are actually only three diphthongs with which you need to concern yourself:

1. *au* (= [a + o], *not* [u]) as in *Frau, Auge, Haus.*

2. *eu, äu* (= [o + e], *not* [i]) as in *Freude, Läuse, heulen.*

3. *ei* (= [a + e], *not* [i]) as in *heiling, leise, ein.*

For the most part, German *consonants* are rather like their English equivalents, with one exception: the set of *sch* sounds. I enjoy beginning articulation with this group because they so visibly reveal the functioning mouth parts. These three sounds, which I like to number in the manner of the French nasals model, are listed below in the order from front to back tongue position:*

1. *Sh* ([ʃ]), spelled *sch* (*schöne*), and initial *s* before *p* and *t* (*Stimme, spüren*).

2. *Forward ch* ([ç]), spelled *ch* (*ich, dich*); *g* after *i* at the end of a word (*richtig*). This is a linguopalatal sound.

3. *Back ch* (ˣ), spelled *ch* after *a, o, au,* or *u* (*doch, dach, Macht, Hauch*). This is a sound formed by the conjunction of the *soft* palate with the back of the tongue, a sort of aspirated hard *g*.

The only other consonant sounds that might offer the non-German speaker some difficulty are [v], [t], [p], and [k].

The [v] sound is spelled *w* as in *Wagner, Wehe, wohin, Löwe,* and *ewig.* Other spellings, rarer, are the *u* after *q* (*quellen, queren*) and the *v* of foreign words only.

The [t] sound is spelled *t* and *tt* (*satt, stehen*) and—note—*d* at the end of a word (*Tod*). The German [t] is voiceless and percussive, as in English.

The [p] sound is spelled *p* and, note, *b* at the end of a word (*ob*).

The [k] sound is spelled generally *k* and *kk* (*klagen, verstehen*), but also as *g* at the end of a word or syllable (*weg, Tag*).

Finally, there are two consonant sounds indigenously German: the [pf]—treated as one sound—and the [ts] sound, spelled *z*. Practice the former on words like *Pferd* and *pfeifen,* flipping the upper lip out as you articulate the labiodental *f*. For the German *z*, make several repetitions of *tse-tse* in front of a mirror; then add vowels.

Some fine points of diction should be mentioned. *G* in

*I am indebted to Frau Belloberg, of the Akademie für Musik in Vienna, for this very helpful paradigm.

German is generally the hard *g*, spelled as *g* or *gg* (*gegen, guten, geben*) and usually soft only in foreign-derived words like *garage*. The [ŋ] sound of the Italian and French *gn* is spelled "backward" in German: that is, *ng*. So pronounce *Singer* as Zi[ŋ]er and not as "Zing͡r." And it's "Henry Kissi[ŋ]er" in German, and not "Henry Kissin[j]er." In sung German, moreover, treat the *l* and *r* exactly as in Italian (Chapter 9).

There is only one glide in German, the [j], which occurs as *i* before another vowel in the ending *ion* (*Nation*), and more frequently before *e* in unstressed syllables where the *e* is a schwa (*Familie*).

A word about doubling. Hand-in-glove with open and closed vowels, consonant doubling affects the meaning as well as the pronunciation of the given word. Doubling the *t* from *bieten* to *bitten* not only changes the vowel from [i] to [I], but it also changes the meaning from "to offer" to "to request." Just remember, then, when doubling: (1) linger slightly on the consonant, and (2) open the vowel.

Finally, we should linger a while on the matter of the *coup de glotte*, the glottal stop. We Americans are especially fond of this type of articulation, evidenced in our daily expressions like "uh-oh." While many great artists exploit the coup de glotte to clarify word meanings or to heighten dramatic tones, it is in my opinion a very harmful ornament, for technical reasons which I'm sure are obvious. If you feel it more "authentic" to employ the coup de glotte, then use it discretely and sparingly.

The sublime miniature of Robert Schumann (1810–1856), *Du bist wie eine Blume* ("Thou Art So Like a Flower"), is a perfect model for our study of German diction (Example 11.1).*

1. Sing the entire *Lied* through on *lu*, repeating for notes and rhythm perfection; for breathing and legato and messa di voce practice; and to resolve any problems in registration and resonation (such as preparing for the *f* at *Gott* in the fourth system).

2. Mark the three *sch* sounds according to the description above. Isolate and practice these words.

3. Circle each schwa. Practice these alone.

*In 56 *Songs You Like to Sing*, pp. 275–276.

Ex. 11.1

Du bist wie eine Blume
Thou art so like a flower

Heinrich Heine

Robert Schumann, Op. 25, No. 24
Composed 1840
Edited by Carl Deis

87700

ist,_____ als ob ich die Hän - de / Auf's Haupt dir le - gen

fain_____ would lay,_ in bless - ing, My hands up - on_____ thy

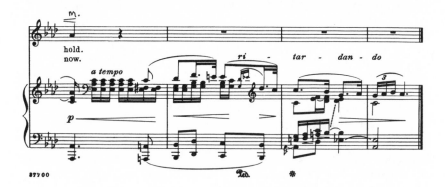

sollt', Be-tend, dass Gott dich er-hal te / So rein und schön und

brow, Pray-ing that God may e'er keepthee As pure and fair as

M.

hold.

now. ri - tar - dan - do

4. Make note of the following references:
   a. Note the difference between the *ie* ([i]) and the diphthong *ei* ([a + e]).
   b. [o] closed; keep the vowel forward and notice what a good vowel for focusing practice this is!
   c. Note the difference in tongue position between *ich* (2) and *schau* (1).
   d. Practice the diphthong [a + o] on *schau*.
   e. Practice the diphthong [a + e] on *schleicht* and note that this word uses both (1) and (2) *sch* sounds.
   f. Sing a voiceless *s* on *ins*.
   g. These are good examples for sostenuto diphthong practice: sustain the [a], close to [en] at the last possible moment.
   h. [p] in *ob*.
   i. *ä* pronounced like [ɛ].
   j. Sustain [a], close to the [o] at the last minute.
   k. Hard *g* in *legen*.
   l. *d* = [t] in *betend*.
   m. *d* = [t] in *hold*.

5. Now speak through the entire poem monotonally, at all times respecting legato and imagining a balance between tone and articulation.

6. Sing the entire *Lied* on one tone, *sostenuto*.

7. Now sing as written, observing dynamics (loud, soft, and varying degrees in between) and other nuances. Present and compare in class.

Now you know the fundamentals of lyric diction in three foreign languages. As we turn now to lyric diction in our mother tongue, don't presume that English diction will be the simplest or most self-evident. You may be in for a surprise, especially as we broach the subject of diphthongs and triphthongs.

Study Questions and Exercises

1. Memorize the three *sch* sounds and corresponding oral formations, and practice in front of a mirror. Compare the forward, middle, and back placement. Then practice these three set, in front of a mirror:

a. (1) = *stille, schöne, mischen, Stuhl, stehen, stören*
b. (2) = *dich, durch* (flipped *r*), *mädchen* (= [mɛt] + [chen]), *mich, reiche, weich*
c. (3) = *Dach, lachen, doch, Buch, Tochter, machen*

Now try this famous Belloberg tongue-twister:

2	1	2	2	3	2	3
"Mädchen,	*schon*	*durch*	*dich*	*dachte*	*ich*	*doch!"*

2. Continue Sieber nos. 25–28. Concentrate on pure vowels, legato, and messa di voce. Become aware of forward and rounded vowels.

3. *Diphthongs:* Practice the following: monotonally:
   a. [a + o]: *Auto, Aussen, Brauhaus, Zauberbaum, Taubenhaus*
   b. [o + e]: *treu, Beutel, Eule, säule, zeugen*
   c. [a + e]: drei, beide, Eile, weinen, Zeit

4. Often "rounding a vowel" is referred to as "umlauting." How does this device compare with the concept of covering? Focus? Relate all of these comparisons to the double-formant concept. How does the umlauting scheme fit in with our seesaw concept?

5. Compare several German songs. What do you notice about legato? That is, in which language, German or, say, Italian, is it easier to sing legato? Why? German and French? Why? German and English? Why? Take a clear look at the vowels in German and Italian: Are the German vowels predominantly more forward or back than those in Italian?

6. Select one of those songs and prepare it for class presentation. Use exactly the same seven-step plan as outlined in this chapter. Make sure you practice in the general progression: (1) technical preparation (breathing, registration, resonation "note learning"); (2) articulation and diction; (3) nuances of dynamics (and later, interpretation); (4) "synthesis," i.e., put it all together in balance.

7. Listen to several recordings of German arias and songs performed by such artists as Hotter, Teyte, Fischer-Dieskau,

Ludwig, Schwarzkopf, Lear, Prey, Schreier, London, Schumann-Heink, Flagstad, Shirley-Quirck, and others. Make observations regarding breathing and legato, range and dynamics, and particularly vowels and resonation. Is legato facilitated or hindered by the consonants? Critique consonant doubling. Compare your opinions in class.

Chapter 12

Summary of English Diction

In America, they haven't used it for years!
— Alan Jay Lerner,
My Fair Lady

VOLUMES COULD BE WRITTEN about the language we take for granted—in fact, several have been.* As with the previous three chapters, this lesson is a summary, limiting itself to four salient points of English diction. The first is an exposure of common diction errors among American singers. The second is the correction of those wrongly learned vowel, consonant, and semiconsonant sounds. A short explanation of diphthongs and triphthongs follows. Finally, we will review the technique of legato singing in English.

Let us begin by reviewing the English vowels. In comparing the following list (Table 12.1) with the German, French, and Italian equivalents, notice the absence of certain pure vowels and the addition of several indigenously English vowel colors:

*Two widely accepted manuals are Madeleine Marshall, *The Singer's Manual of English Diction* (New York: Schirmer Books, 1953), and Dorothy Uris, *To Sing in English* (New York: Boosey and Hawkes, 1971).

TABLE 12.1

ah group	[ɑ] as in *father* [æ] as in *cat* [a] as in *task* [ɒ] as in *hot* [ɔ] as in *warm*
ay group	[ɛ] as in *wed* [ɜ] as in *learn* [ə] as in *sofa*
ee group	[i] as in *me* [I] as in *hit*
oh group	[o] as in *obey* [ʌ] as in *upon*
oo group	[u] as in *too* [U] as in *full*

Standing in front of a mirror, practice each group. Memorize the sensation and sight of each proper pronunciation. Despite visual and oral correctness, nevertheless, you may still be guilty of an American flaw: the "twang," or hypernasality. For by-now-obvious reasons, you will want to tip the balance toward the large throat in that event, especially on the front vowels and their variations. Such gestures reinforce the importance of possessing the ability to sing pure [u] and remind us of its major role in resonance and placement. Listening to American singers across the country, you will harvest a range of impure [u]'s from the East Coast diphthongs (e.g., [æ + o]) to the California [ʌ] and [ə].

Another pronunciation flaw, endemic to American colloquial language, is the "American r." Not only is the sound offensive to the ear, its production is just bad vocal technique. To illustrate, never let "w[ɜ]sh[I]p" become "w[ɜ]rrsh[I]p." Keep that distinction in mind as you say the following: *earth, bird, her, myrtle.* Omit the r altogether in [ɔ] words such as *lord, warm,* and *morn.*

[I] and [i] are often carelessly slung around in everyday speech. As a rule, words such as *divine* and *beautiful* employ the open [I] sound. Do not overcompensate, nevertheless, by confusing [I] with [i] in words such as *fillings* and *still*, both [I].

In answer to the confusion over [æ] versus [a] words, and [u] versus the glide [yu], Madeleine Marshall offers two handy schemes (pp. 116 ff.). The first is the collection of "ask" words. With respect to the first controversy, Miss Marshall's general rule is to use the [a] pronunciation for words with one of seven endings:

1. [f]   as in *half, calf, laugh*

2. *nce*   as in *chance* (with exceptions)

3. *nche*   as in *blanche, avalanche*

4. *s–*   as in *ask, fast*

5. *th*   as in *bath, hath, wrath*

6. *nt*   as in *chant, can't*

7. *mand*   as in *reprimand, demand* (a rare form)

The other capsulization is the so-called "Daniel Sitteth" group, whose title is fleshed out from its constituent consonants. In these words, the [yu] glide is preferred over the pure [u], after:

1. *d*   as in *duty, induce, during*

2. *n*   as in *new, nuisance, neurotic*

3. *l*   as in *lute, prelude* (exception: [u], when a non-*l* consonant precedes the *l*, as in *blue*)

4. *s*   as in *suitor, ensure, pursue*

5. *t*   as in *Tuesday, student, restitution*

6. *th* as in *enthusiasm*

Review the consonants in English by first rehearsing them as outlined in Chapter 8. Then examine Table 12.2, which is set up according to functioning mouth part and production as voiced or voiceless.* Begin to be aware of the "new" consonant

*For a complete description of English consonants, see Uris, pp. 164 ff.

TABLE 12.2

Voiced		Voiceless	
	Labials		
b	as in *beauty*	*p*	as in *piano*
w	as in *word*	[hw]	as in *whisper*
m	as in *music*		
	Labiodentals		
v	as in *vibrator*	*f*	as in *function*
	Linguodentals		
th	as in *breathing*	*th*	as in *theme*
z	as in *zeal*	*s*	as in *sound*
s [ʒ]	as in *measure*	*sh*	as in *shape*
d	as in *drill*	*t*	as in *but*
n	as in *nasal*		
l	as in *link*		
j	as in *jar* (and soft *g*—*gesture*)	*ch*	*as in chance*
r	(flipped) as in *rest*		
	Linguopalatals		
g	as in *glide*	*k*	as in *key*
y	as in *yawm*		
ng [ŋ]	as in *sing*		

sounds (such as the voiced and voiceless *th*), and the proper execution with lips, tongue, and teeth, as you practice in front of a mirror, noting the common errors in production.

What we have called in other languages "semiconsonants," we call in English diction "semivowels." (I am reminded of the proverbial inquiry about the cocktail glass: Is it half empty or half full?) There are three semivowels in English: [r], [w], and [y].

The [r] is closely allied with the [ʒ] sound, pronounced *ur*. It appears in nine different forms in English. As an initial consonant, for example in the word *rose*, pronounce the *r* as a semivowel glide into the succeeding sound, a vowel. (However, in pure "Queen's English," flip the *r* slightly.)

Closely tied to this rule is the one for initial *r* in an unstressed syllable (e.g., *arise*). Use the same rules as for an initial consonant.

Between words, r is never stressed. Treat it as an elision, virtually unpronounced ("roar of . . .").

Flip the r that follows initial consonants (e.g., *breath, bring*).

We come here to the important category Miss Marshall calls the "morning glory" r's. These are formed with trumpet-shaped lips. Avoid either extreme of the flipped r or the American ɝ·rr as you practice these vocables: *turn, word, virtue, learn, bird, earth, pursue, further, worship.*

The r in an unstressed schwa syllable resembles the "morning glory" approach, but exacts even less of the r coloring. Think of the syllable as predominately [ə] with words like *father, honor*, and *letter*.

After vowels the r is a semivowel which slightly colors the vowels. Never extend the r color into the succeeding consonant in such words as *mortal* and *darling*, where it colors the preceding vowel.

The final occurrence of r as a semivowel is in words like *pair, peer*, and *poor*. These are correctly sung as two syllables, with the second syllable sounding as an unstressed schwa.*

The second semivowel glide is the [w] sound, a voiced glide related to pure [u]. Note that [w] is never voiced in the final position, and is in fact silent in words such as *sorrow* and *window*. The [w] is formed with rounded lips and is pronounced as a glide into the succeeding sound, always a vowel. *With*, for example, is the glide [w] into [I] plus the voiceless *th*. To keep this discipline in line with good posture, form the lips for [u] first, then phonate to the "point" of the vowel, thus circumventing the common fault of scooping, both ascending and descending, as the glide to the vowel. Never substitute [w] for [hw], so that you say *witch* when you mean *which*. To be on the safe side, take care to accompany [hw] with a slight puff of air on the exhalation.

Third is the [y] glide, related to the [i] vowel. It is a voiced semivowel, a branch of the "Daniel Sitteth" glides. Like the [w], the [y] is never found in the final position in words like *happy* or *fury*. Practice forming this glide in front of a mirror. It is shaped

---

*This rule is not universally accepted for such vocables as *fair, wear, pair*, etc. You may prefer the alternative [ɛə] pronunciation for these.

by the sides of the tongue and the hard palate, like a rounded [i].
As you pass on to the succeeding sound, a vowel, the tongue
moves quickly forward into the vowel. Practice on *you, yes, yawn,*
and *year.* In any event, do not tolerate guttural scoops, and never
substitute Americanisms like *ch,* for example, for the glide [y]
("can't you," for example, and not "can-chew.").

Our diphthongs and triphthongs are more elusive than you
might imagine. Did you know, for example, that our equivalent
of the pure [e] is not [ɛi], but [ɛI]? Our first rule for these vowel
combinations, then, is to always honor both (or all three)
components of the vowel cluster. Secondly—and you have
heard this before—in sostenuto singing of diphthongs and
triphthongs, sustain the primary vowel and close to the
secondary vowel only at the last moment (hence "now" =
naaa-u).

Thirdly, in the matching of speech and tone, known as
declamation, be sure not to stress unimportant components of
the diphthongs and triphthongs. Even if the composer has set it
incorrectly, sing the text as if you were speaking it ("people" in
Handel's "Comfort Ye," for example, is *not* pi-o-ple!)

As you study the following groups of diphthongs and
triphthongs, practice each syllable slowly in front of a mirror,
recalling all of our previous discussion about vowels. Speak,
then sing them, observing the rules for sostenuto treatment of
diphthongs and triphthongs:*

1. Diphthongs ending in [I], not [i]
   a. [ɑI] as in *buy, high, like, might*
   b. [əI] as in *joy, voice, oil, boy*
   c. [ɛI] as in *bay, may, place, afraid*

2. Diphthongs ending in [ɜ]
   a. [Iɜ] as in *fear, year, hear, appear*
   b. [ɛɜ] as in *fair, bear, their, prayer*
   c. [ɑɜ] as in *far, arm, depart, heart*
   d. [ɔɜ] as in *for, scorn, storm, war*
   e. [oɜ] as in *pore, before, mourn, report*
   f. [Uɜ] as in *poor, your,* and [yu] glides *surely, pure*

*An excellent, fully detailed account of diphthongs and triphthongs can be
found in Lloyd Pfautsch, *English Diction for Singers* (New York: Lawson-Gould
Music Publishers, 1971), pp. 49–77.

3. Diphthongs ending in [u]
    a. [ɑu] as in *now, out, thou, louder*
    b. [ou] as in *no, own, show, ghost*
    c. [iu] This basically is the same as the Daniel Sitteth glide as in *new* (hence *b* as in *beautiful* could be added to our D.S. list)

The two triphthongs may be treated in the same manner as the diphthongs:

1. [ɑI3] as in *tire, desire, fire, choir, triumph* (compare these with the *r*-schwa treatment above)

2. [ɑu3] as in *tower, our, flower, power*

Do not ignore legato in your articulation and vowel endeavors. Remember that hand-in-glove with breathing, legato is the foundation of your vocal technique and the sine qua non of artistic singing. In practicing legato singing in English, keep in mind these maxims:

1. Legato in English is the connection of tone syllables. Review Chapter 8 for their definition and for the articulation-tone balance.

2. Think of legato as the relay-race metaphor described in Chapter 2.

3. Legato is neither "smearing" (weak consonants) nor detached (percussive consonants that break up the line), but a balance of lips-tongue-teeth-throat versus tone.

4. At this juncture you can incorporate other practices from other languages, such as the French liaisons, into your concept of legato. Do so now.

5. Remember that "consonant" literally means "sounds with." That meaning implies that good diction and legato in English require pure consonants sounding with (not against) pure vowels.

6. A final word on the plosives (*p,t,k,b,d,g*) comes from Uris (p. 60): "To preserve unbroken *legato*: prepare the vowel in advance, and then in one movement, deliver it together

> with the consonant in a single pattern holding the jaw steady. . . . Plosives are . . . produced in the shape of the following vowel."

To tie together our exposition on vowels, semivowels, consonants, diphthongs, triphthongs, and legato, let us examine an excerpt from an Arcadian aria by G. F. Handel (1685–1750), "Where'er You Walk."* The excerpt (Example 12.1) is the "B" section of the da capo aria, the predominant form for Italian arias of the Baroque.

Practice this excerpt along these suggested lines:

1. Sing the entire excerpt through on *lu,* still observing correct breathing (especially in the rests) and legato; note the rhythm on the first *you,* and *flourish,* and perhaps try out a messa di voce on the sustained notes (e.g., *all,* m. 4). Anticipate registration difficulties such as occur in the last two measures of the excerpt.

2. Don't assume you know the correct pronunciation for the vowels and diphthongs. Doublecheck the following, indicated with lower-case letters in the score:
   a. Like *fair,* is either [ɛɜ] or [ɛə].
   b. Same as a.
   c. Like *now,* is [ɑu].
   d. Like *buy,* is [ɑI]. Sustain the [ɑ].
   e. Like *morning glory, learn,* is [ɜ].
   f. Same as e.
   g. Like *poor,* is [Uɜ]. Sustain the [U].

All others are pure [u], [ɛ], various *ah* vowels, and [ə] on *the.*

3. Now practice some consonants in front of a mirror:
   a. The *r* group: review the difference between the semivowel and the consonant *r* in such words as *where, tread, flourish.* There are 21 examples of *r* in this excerpt alone!

*From his opera *Semele.* The entire aria can be found in *56 Songs You Like to Sing,* pp. 195–196.

   b. Practice the remaining consonants, observing the
      mouth parts utilized:
      (1) *tr*
      (2) *bl*
      (3) *t* initial
      (4) *d* final (avoid guttural scoop)
      (5) [y] glide on *you, your* (review execution)
      (6) [hw]
      (7) *n* and *ng* as glides (note how these aid in
          forward brilliance and placement)

4. Mark and drill on the elisions and tone syllables for legato
   practice. Sing each phrase on one note sostenuto.

5. Whisper the whole excerpt as if singing legato.

6. Sing the whole excerpt on vowels only, musically as
   written, sostenuto, and *mp* dynamic level.

7. Now sing through the entire piece as written, summing
   up all of steps 1–6. Observe legato line, clear articulation,
   correct vowel formation, proper placement, good breathing and registration technique. Memorize. Present in
   class.

A rigorous schedule like the above may strike you as onerous
and perhaps even a little fussy, at first. Because it is so thorough,
however, it will save you many hours of unnecessary frustra-
tion in undoing wrongly learned habits later. You may discover,
too, that without such a vigorous routine, your English
selections may be regarded as your dullest.
We are now prepared to shift to yet another level of growth
in this study. You have studied a great deal about tone and
articulation and have a reasonable awareness of diction in four
languages. That diction discipline serves, moreover, as a bridge
to the noblest function in singing, itself a bridge from singing as
a *skill* to singing as an *art*. That discipline is the *art of interpretation*.

Study Questions and Exercises

1. One of the most telltale faults in American diction is the
   "American r." Review all possibilities regarding the pronun-

Ex. 12.1

Where'er you walk

Aria from "Semele"

Edited by H. Heale

G. F. Händel

ciation of *r* and correct any bad habits, if applicable. Note well the vocables with *r* before *t, d, l,* and the nasal sounds. Concentrate your drill on these.

2. Do the same with the Americanisms on *but* and *had* (final consonant replaced by glottal stop). What is the error in diction? In phonation and the large throat? Comment on the American treatment of the hard *g.*

3. Practice all diphthongs and triphthongs. Keep a list of those you have mislearned and continue practicing until you have adjusted them. Give particular attention to those which occur in words using the semivowel *r.*

4. Continue with Sieber nos. 29–32. Practice vowels as Italian, and consonants as (1) Italian and (2) English. Concentrate on resonance and vowels, legato and breathing, and registration and vowels.

5. Compare several American and English songs. First examine them, just from the standpoint of consonant study. Which consonants predominate in English? What position (initial, middle, final) predominates? What are the predominant consonants in terms of tongue-placement (i.e., tongue-teeth, tongue-palate, tongue-throat)? Comment on legato singing in English.

6. Select one of those songs for presentation in class. (You may wish to choose a popular song, but you will find that it is frequently more difficult to achieve a legato line with these than with art songs and arias). Prepare this selection exactly as outlined in the last part of this chapter.

7. Listen to several recordings of English and American arias and songs performed by such artists as Baker, Price, Lear, McCormack, Lewis, Pears, Gramm, Shirley-Quirk, Horne, Sills, Sutherland, Treigle, and others. Make observations regarding treatment of the diphthongs and triphthongs, legato line, "Daniel Sitteth" words, treatment of the *r* sounds, and the balance of tone and articulation.

Chapter 13

On Interpretation

Your interpretation is moulded by your emotion which welds imagination and thought together.

—G. P. Lamperti,
Vocal Wisdom

GLANCING BACK, you realize that we have moved from an analysis of tone and articulation through the region of diction and now are ready to embark on a study of the most intimate of the functions in vocal technique, the art of interpretation.

Interpretation can be generally defined as the personal and creative element in the performance of music which, as in drama, depends on a middleman between the composer and the audience: the performer. This performer, if he or she is to be a noted interpreter, must extend himself or herself beyond the level of virtuosity and sheer technical brilliance to a level equal to that of the work's creation.

It is the performer who must transform the composer's work from the printed page into vital communication. . . . The ideal performer is one who succeeds in bestowing on a composition a personal and original expression *within the stylistic frame* of the work and *in full compliance with the intentions indicated by the composer.**

Implicit in this approach to interpretation is an important principle: to be an interpreter the performer must take pains to study historical and formal style analysis in addition to formal technical training.

For singers, the interpretative process is unique, for it demands the understanding of both musical and poetic symbols, in addition to historical and formal details.

Ultimately our goal in vocal interpretation, as Pierre Bernac relates, is the welding of the two meanings, music and text (1972, p. 3):

> In order to do full justice to vocal music, each sound must have its value, not only in pitch and rhythm, but also in color and verbal stress. . . . The music of the poem is as important as the music set *to* the poem. The music of the words and the music itself are one and the same; they should not be disassociated.

You see, although it is a wonderful thrill to witness the pyrotechnics of a masterful coloratura, or a sublime titillation to experience the subtle *voix mixte* of a cultured baritone, the *art* of singing demands more. Beyond the realm of breathing, registration, resonation, and diction is a higher achievement: interpretation. In the words of the great German prima donna, Lotte Lehman (1945, pp. 10, 12):

> Certainly, no one can question that technique is the all-important foundation—the a,b,c's of singing. . . . But realize that technique must be mastered to the point of being *unconscious,* before you can become an interpreter. . . . Like a frame, music encloses the word picture—and now comes your interpretation, breathing life into this work of art, welding word and tone with equal feeling into one whole, so that the poet sings and the composer becomes poet, and two arts are born again as one. . . .

The vocal interpreter must also seek out those from whom he can glean the musical traditions—those nuances and embellishments passed on from the first generation of interpreters down to the present. These traditions embody subtleties

---

*See Willi Apel, ed., *The Harvard Dictionary of Music* (Cambridge, Mass.: Harvard University Press, 1960), "Expression," "Interpretation," pp. 302, 418. Italics added.

such as cadenzas, certain shadings in tempo and line, and shapings in phrases.*

At the highest level the interpreter will find himself embracing a world of character depiction, a *je ne sais quoi* I prefer to call artistic soul. For when music and poem fuse in that heavenly moment of performance, something beyond that musical moment governs the music rhythm. The audience can sense it even before the first utterance, in the very countenance of a great artist.

We actually feel the presence of this spirit in the soul of the live performance. It cannot be taught. It must be personally developed. It is your goal as an interpreter, and the end-point of this chapter.

How do seasoned singers go about "working up" an interpretation? Can we devise a plan or method to follow, as we did in the chapters on technical development?

There is no all-inclusive program for evolving an interpretation—the process is too intimate to lend itself to generalization. Following the lead given by great teachers of the past, perhaps it would be most efficacious to demonstrate the "working out" of an interpretation by example. Our example for this exposition is the famous ballad written in 1815 by Franz Schubert (1797–1828), *Erlkönig* ("The Erl-King.")† We will start at the juncture between technical perfection and the beginning of the interpretative phase; that is, let us assume the music has been learned and the technical matters have been perfected.

Paralleling the technical program, I would like to offer here a seven-staged procedure for studying and interpreting *Erlkönig* (the score is given in Example 13.1).

Step 1. *The first step in interpretation is a literal (as opposed to poetic) translation of the text. You will want to write in the word-for-word*

---

*Such nuances require an ability in word coloring and chiaroscuro, for which you will want to review Chapters 3 and 7. The technique of characterization, which will be explained in this chapter, cannot be approached without a secure foundation in the resonance and agility techniques described in those two chapters.

†I highly recommend that in conjunction with this study you listen to the exceptional interpretation by Hermann Prey. Play the recording several times to appreciate his artistic handling of timbre variations and characterization.

English translation under the German in your score. Here is my literal translation of the Goethe original:

1. *Who rides so late through night and wind?*
    It is the father *and his* son.
    He has the child (engulfed) completely in his arms;
    He grasps him securely; he holds him warmly.

2. *"My son, why do you hide your face so fearfully?"*
    "Don't you see, Father, (see) the Erl-King—
    The Erl-King with his crown and train?"
    "My son, it is only a ribbon of fog."

3. *"You lovely child, come, go with me!*
    Such pretty games I will play with you.
    Multicolored flowers are (growing) on the strand.
    My mother has many a golden garment."

4. *"My father! My father! Do you not hear*
    What the Erl-King is softly promising me?"
    "Be still, stay calm, my son.
    In the dry leaves, the wind is whispering."

5. *"Do you, my fine lad, want to go with me?*
    My daughters will wait on you (so) nicely;
    My daughters are leading the great dance,
    And they will rock, and dance, and sing you to sleep."

6. *"My father! My father! And do you not see there,*
    The Erl-King's daugthers in that distant place?"
    "My son! My son! I see it clearly;
    The old willows are glowing so grisly."

7. *"I love you, your beautiful mien excites me,*
    But if you are not willing, I will have to use force!"
    "My father! My father! Now he seizes me!
    The Erl-King has hurt me!"

8. *The father shudders; he rides hurriedly,*
    He holds in his arms the moaning child.
    Just now he arrives at the courtyard,
    (When) In his arms, the child . . . was dead.

Step 2. *Study the characters.* As you study the portrayal of each character, be conscious of potential vocal colors and musical depictions of the character. Mark each entrance (with N, S, E, or F for the narrator, son, Erl-King, father, respectively), and analyze each character individually.

Narrator:

This character, who stands to one side of the "stage" like a seventeeth-century *testo,* frames the entire story from beginning to end. Color him with a straightforward tone rather like a storyteller or even a modern-day commentator. The first stanza should do little more dramatically than set the scene. With the return of the narrator (stanza 8) the character loses some of his "distance" from the drama, though. The rests that perforate the key dramatic line (at *Hof, Müh,* and *Not)* create an agitated, breathless air in the diction. I would aim for a stage-whisper effect—still, of course, within the context of the Lieder limitations Do not by shy about taking the fermata over the rest quite literally (at *war tot);* this is a dramatic, and not strictly musical, direction.

Son:

If one affect sums up this character, it is fear. Even with the first utterance of the son, there should be a tremor in the voice, an excitement that builds to out-and-out terror in stanza 7. To depict the frightened, youthful quality of the son, I would choose a timbre balanced toward the "white" end of the spectrum and even give it a somewhat breathy texture. At all events, you will want to create a *poco a poco crescendo* of fear from stanza 2 through stanza 7. It is not clear after this stanza whether the boy is dead at this point, one of those marvelous ambiguities poets of Goethe's genius revel in. Regardless of your interpretation of this point, remember, it is the narrator who has the last word and who must sustain the suspense until *war tot.*

Erl-King:

How should we view this personage? Is he the personification of Death? Or perhaps the Devil? No matter how you imagine this character, I am sure we can agree that he is a sinister, Bosch-like, otherwordly personage. His taunts range from the seductive sneering of the third stanza to the near demonic forcefulness of stanza 7.

Of all four roles, the Erl-King demands the greatest range of vocal colors. Initially, you will want to execute an eerie, leering, high-pitched sound, a sneering essence in stanza 3. To that effect, you may exaggerate the "forward brilliance" by playing on the high-formant vowels, such as the [i] of *liebes* and [e] of *geh*. It is as if you are singing on your teeth.

In an abrupt change of tactics, the Erl-King suddenly turns "chatty" in stanza 5. Keep this patter lightly on the tongue and teeth, and don't fight the cross-rhythm with the accompaniment. This rhythmic ambiguity heightens the "busy-ness" of the character.

Just as abruptly the Erl-King loses patience in stanza 7. Out of an almost erotic fever he suddenly plunges into a near-shouted ejaculation at *Gewalt!* You cannot exaggerate the articulation at this point, nor be too "heavy." Let the listener know the true character of the Erl-King as he forcefully yanks the boy at *Gewalt*.

Father:

Here is the central figure of the drama, the liaison between the son and the Erl-King. As interpreters we must study his dialogue as reactions to the outer stimuli and reflections of his inner conflict between fear and paternal protectiveness. In that light, study the transformation of his character from the ill-at-ease but comforting parent at the onset of the ballad to the emotionally spent *rôle pathétique* in the courtyard.

To portray this range of emotions, you will want to set clearly in your mind various vocal colors. Maintain a veil of warmth, in the colors of a late Rembrandt painting, throughout the *Lied*. Against this posture in stanza 4 you will want to convey a nervous tremor—a conflict between the rational and emotional elements. At stanza 6, where the father, too, sees the apparitions, show fear and even a little curiosity in the voice, still veiled in the "mellow resonance" of warmth and masculinity.

Step 3. Practice the characterizations in this sequence:

a. Sing each character separately, working up a distinct

tone quality and mood for each character within each stanza, and then in succession.

b. Memorize the lines for each character, as you would for a stage play. Practice, speaking aloud, the dialogue for each role by heart.

c. Speak through the entire poem, from memory, attending to the difficult, sudden shifts of character and mood.

d. Repeat the second and third steps as sung dialogue. Concentrate on character depiction and timbre variation.

Step 4. For subtlety of interpretation, focus on certain words to be colored and stressed. For example, here are nine words which are keys to bringing the characters in *Erlkönig* to life:

a. *liebes*, m. 58: use high-formant [i], nasal to create a sneering effect.

b. *spiel*, m. 64: alter the [i] from "sneering" to a rounded, playful color.

c. *Vater*, m. 72: in this and the remaining dialogue of the son, exaggerate all [f] attacks, almost as if inhaling on the attack itself.

d. *ruhig*, m. 81: What a perfectly onomatopoetic word to emphasize the "mellowness" of the father character—a natural low-formant [u]. Make the vowel spacious and warm.

e. stanza 5, mm. 86 ff.: Keep all consonants "on the teeth" and "forward," thereby underscoring the "chatty" quality.

f. *liebe*, m. 117: treat this [i] again as in m. 58.

g. *Gewalt*, m. 123: let yourself create a hoarse, shouting quality, a flat [ɑ] with a barking quality on the [g] and [v] sounds.

h. *grauset's*, m. 134: let the [o] of the diphthong hollow in a cavernous pharyngeal space, trembling with ominous expectation.

i. *war tot*, m. 147: clearly, these two words are the focal point of the entire drama. Treat them in a quasi–stage whisper. Since all that precedes is an emotional crescendo to the word *tot*, take as much time as needed for the effect (and note that

Schubert, rhythmically speaking, has virtually suspended this cell in midair).

Step 5. Analyze the piano accompaniment for any salient motives—musical syllables used for character and drama symbolism. Clearly the piano part is a spinning out of the octave iteration (r.h.) + arsis-thesis motive (l.h.) in mm. 1–2.

Think of this *Fortspinnung* theme as the horse. Its variations thus appear as the "anxious charge" (mm. 1–54); the "galloping pacer" (mm. 58–72); the "stomping steed" (mm. 72–81); the "posting stallion" (mm. 87–96); again the "stomping steed" (mm. 96–105); the return of the "anxious charge" (mm. 112–116); then a state of "collection" (mm. 116–123); a repeat of the "stomping steed" (mm. 123–131); and finally a variation of the original "anxious charge."

Isolate the left-hand permutations, and treat them as depictions of the varying moods of the Erl-King. See especially the conspicuous mood shifts at mm. 96 ff. and mm. 112 ff.

Step 6. Examine the score for salient historical and formal elements that contribute to an interpretation.

Study the dynamics as musical elements to be memorized, noting as you do the wide range from *ppp* (87 ff.) to the telling *fff* at *Gewalt*. Draw a parallel between dynamics and character. For example, until the Erl-King reveals his true nature at m. 123, he exudes softspoken tones. By contrast, the son is shaded by a heave-ho of dynamic contrasts.

In the realm of harmonic analysis, *Erlkönig* reflects the Romantic penchant for *mood* as mode—*mod*-ulation as *mood* change. The entire ballad is circumscribed by the sombre G minor mode. Our concern here is where it deviates from G minor. As you mark these modulation points in your score, be thinking of an answer to the question, "Why *this* modulation—what does it symbolize?" There are five significant modulations in *Erlkönig:*

a. m. 26, at *Knaben*
b. m. 54, at *Nebelstreif*

c. m. 58 and ff., the entire Erl-King dialogue
d. m. 88 and ff., the entire Erl-King dialogue
e. m. 116 and ff., the entire Erl-King dialogue

Look at all those Erl-King dialogues written in the *major mode!* But the Erl-King, we agree, is a sinister character and should be portrayed in *minor mode* . . . unless he is not being true to his character. . . . Do you see how *harmony* helps to tell the story?

Melodically, we need to touch briefly on an area known as "performance practices." Specifically, we want to determine how to treat the little notes called *appoggiaturas.* Here are my suggestions, based on musicological research and contemporary custom:

a. m. 26: could be either C = half note or C = quarter note, B$^\flat$ = quarter note. I choose the latter.
b. m. 28: same as a.
c. m. 30: same as a.
d. m. 64: Here we have an in-written ornamentation, called in modern theory a "double auxiliary." It is a "playful" motive decorating the word *Spiel.*
e. m. 134: one quarter-note each on A and G.
f. m. 138: one quarter-note each on E$^\flat$ and D.

Now let us inspect the rhythmic and metric elements of *Erlkönig.* These elements are used as character motives, just like those of harmony and melody. For example, look at the two-against-three rhythmic conflict between melody and accompaniment in the fifth stanza (mm. 86 ff.). The "busy" effect will not be obtained if the 4/4 meter in the vocal line is anything less than strict.

Have you noticed the *accelerando* at m. 135? Here Schubert clearly intends to modify the word *geschwind,* so do move it along.

What sort of rhythmic pattern suits a narrator better than a free recitative? And it is precisely that pattern in which our narrator concludes the ballad. Sing the recitative ending, therefore, relatively unmeasured, within the matrix of a storytelling scene, give the impression that the narrator is "closing the book," removing his glasses, as it were, and uttering with fateful finality, *war tot.*

Lastly in our historical-formal analysis, let us make a cursory inspection of the *shape* of *Erlkönig*—form in the conventional sense.* This *Lied* is of the *ballad* genre—an "open" or "through-composed" form. That is, its form is devoid of sectional repeats, consisting rather of a string of dialogues: A–B–C–D, etc. This form ideally suits a storytelling text, where there is no need to contrast similar sections. In short, keep surging forward to the climactic *war tot*.

The tiny musical interludes are your only opportunity to shift moods and character. I would isolate these little transitions and practice them solely for purposes of character and mood shifts.

Step 7. Our last step is one of synthesis. Reweave all six steps, and then "run it." That is, sing *Erlkönig* nonstop, with accompaniment, from first note to last, and repeat until fluent.

These are the elements of interpretation that can be practiced, with a progressive plan for doing so. We have yet another aspect of interpretation to attend to: that elusive *je ne sais quoi*. What is this *je ne sais quoi?*

Perhaps it is a mortal reflection of rhythm, the Divine Tactus.

While singing is the fusion of tone and poem, the song it creates is brought to life by that heavenly heartbeat, rhythm. At a fundamental, primordial level, music is rhythm, just as at the same level drama is rhythm. The moment of an artistic utterance in song merges the earthbound and the infinite as it fuses poem and tone into one artistic unity. At that instant the song is thus transformed into a union of pulse and personality, of line and color.

Without pulse—music-rhythm—there is no line, no legato, no continuity. Without personality—lyric-rhythm—there is no color, no shading, no contrast.

*It is my contention that knowing the form of a piece is an aid in memorization. If you know, for example, that the aria to be memorized is a *da capo* aria (ABA'), you can be encouraged that having committed the A-section to memory, you have virtually memorized two-thirds of the aria.

Ex. 13.1

The Erl-King.
(ERLKÖNIG.)

FR. SCHUBERT.

6535

6535

nächt - li-chen Reih'n und wie - gen und tan - zen und sin - gen dich ein,   sie

wie - gen und tan - zen und sin - gen dich ein."   „Mein Va - ter, mein

Va - ter,   und siehst du nicht dort   Erl - kö-nigs Töch-ter am   dü - stern

decresc.

Ort?"   „Mein Sohn,   mein Sohn,   ich seh' es ge-

6535

nau, es scheinen die al - ten Wei - den so grau."

"Ich lie - be dich, mich reizt dei - ne schö - ne Ge -

stalt; und bist du nicht wil - lig, so brauch ich Ge - walt." "Mein Va - ter, mein

Va - ter, jetzt fasst er mich an! Erl - kö - nig hat mir ein

Thus it is that in the act of the singing art, poetic drama bathes us in an aura of psychic colors and shades, all the while creating a living chiaroscuro about the very lines of our own rhythm.

Study Questions and Exercises

1. Many times after a singer has worked out his or her interpretation, he or she has less difficulty with the technical demands of the piece than before, even though little technical work has been done in the process. Why do you suppose this phenomenon occurs, psychologically?

2. Draw a parallel between vowel resonance and timbre as a technique and what Bernac calls "verbal stress." Draw the same sort of parallel between breathing skills and what Lotte Lehmann terms the "gasping-exhaustion" (p. 27) motives at the conclusion of *Erlkönig*. Draw a third equation between registration and range, and the characterization of the son in *Erlkönig*.

3. It is likely that Schubert wanted the major mode in mm. 141–146 to convey a feeling of finality, a "last-ditch" effort on the part of the father. List your interpretations of the other five appearances of the major mode in *Erlkönig*.

4. Study Sieber nos. 33–36. Review legato singing, and all exercises in breathing, registration, and resonation. Practice arbitrarily coloring various vowels. Explore dynamic contrast. Try out tempo variations such as *accelerando* and *ritardando,* and make note of the effect of those variations on breath management. Work with an accompanist, if possible, and make some observations about dynamics and balance.

5. Listen to several recordings of *Erlkönig* to compare and critique in terms of interpretive thoroughness and depth of characterization (to suggest a few: Prey, Fischer-Dieskau, Hotter, Flagstad, Lehmann, Adam, Shirley-Quirk). Disregard any technical considerations in your critique, unless the technical element in one way or another affects the interpretation.

6. Choose an art song (or aria) for presentation in class. Prepare it technically as before. Then analyze and rehearse your selection along the lines of the seven-tiered program in this chapter. Sing the piece by heart—remember that knowing the form will aid in memorization.

7. Interpretation is individual. Listen to several recordings by several individuals singing the same piece. Write down how they differ interpretatively and how they are similar. Also include your opinion as to whether certain differences are acceptable (i.e., within the framework of the formal and historical requisites and traditions, and in compliance with the composer's original intentions) or unacceptable. Justify your opinions with examples from the music, complemented, if possible, by remarks written by the composer himself.

Chapter 14

The Synthesis
of Habits

*Never disassociate these three—word, tone, and breath. . . . The
union of this trinity is like three children playing in a ring, holding
hands. If one lets go, all are helpless.*

—G. B. Lamperti,
Vocal Wisdom

AT THIS STAGE in your vocal development it should
be clear that singing—the technique and the art—is composed
of many little dynamic functions, each of which demands its
own discipline and development. The final fruition of the
singing discipline is that dynamic balance we have described
earlier as the *cantus lībrātus* in the act of performance.

The final step in our program of vocal development, and a
bridge to the fully developed cantus lībrātus, is the *synthesis of
habits.*

This notion is not original with me but is the property of the
distinguished dean, George Howerton, who describes the
synthesis of habits as a process

> in which a number of individual components enter to make a total
> response. A singer's effectiveness largely depends upon the
> degree to which he is able to combine these diversified constituents
> into a unified reaction. . . . As long as the singer must give

conscious attention to any one of the separate aspects of the singing process, he is unable to achieve a performance that is fully rounded and complete.*

To be freed of that conscious, voluntary attention to the habits of singing—a freedom without which the involuntary cantus lībrātus cannot occur—requires an assessment and adjustment of the habits in a less dynamic state. That assessment, a diagnostic program for weighing and adjusting, is a process known as coordination.

Our checklist for coordination reveals that we are no strangers to balance. On one level, we know that we must balance breathing, registration, and resonation habits. For example, we know that faulty breathing can create tension, which will have an immediate negative effect on the production of "high notes" (affecting registration) and inhibit "ring" and "projection" (affecting resonation). A defective registration technique can cause breath management to suffer, consequently limiting vowel resonance. And errors in "placement" and ring can negatively influence register adjustments and thereby disrupt "support" and "breath control."

At this level of coordination, a good tool for diagnosis and regulation is the effective vocalise devised by William Vennard, the "yawn-sigh." I present this tool with some reservations, for, like the messa di voce, the yawn-sigh can develop the voice or damage it, depending on its execution and its supervision. Therefore, always practice the yawn-sigh under the supervision of an experienced teacher, and only then.

I would suggest you consult Vennard's description (p. 211) to supplement mine, just to be on the safe side. My definition is a simple, two-step procedure (in front of a mirror, of course):

Step 1. As a preliminary gesture, swivel your neck to release neck tension while you form a comfortable *ah** with the jaw loose and hanging freely.

---

*I prefer the Italian [ɑ] for this exercise; others prefer [a]. Either is acceptable so long as the tongue is relaxed and the throat is free and open.

Step 2. Remembering that this exercise encourages the freedom and open throat of a yawn, and the absolutely light adjustment of a sigh, attack on *ah* in the upper register while simulating a yawn. Use good breath management as you descend in pitch (and increase the "weight" as you near the primary passagio).

Now here are some important don't's with the yawn-sigh:

1. Never *knödel* (overly cover) the vowel.

2. Avoid jaw motion and shoulder motion as you descend.

3. Never allow the neck to stiffen.

4. If you have difficulty initiating the attack in the high register, try attacking on [k] and modifying the vowel toward [o]. But if you use the consonant for the attack, remember: this must be a pure tongue back-velum [k] and not a guttural [ʌk] or [ŋk].

5. Never gawk (i.e., distend your neck) on the attack.

6. Never allow the throat to pinch or close, especially on entering the low register.

7. Never force the sound or shove; rather "drink in" the tone.

At the next level in coordination, we want to equalize the components of tone and articulation. You will want to make sure that one doesn't overpower the other—that diction does not constrain free tone or that mellowness is not "mushing" the diction. This means checking that you haven't lost your good resonation in your efforts to clearly articulate, for example. By the same token, you will not want to be one of those unfortunates about whom it is opined, "What a magnificent voice! Couldn't understand a word, though."

On a still higher level in our balance check, we will want to symmetrize the dimension of technique versus interpretation. At this level I can only offer vague guidelines, since the art of interpretation is so personal. Basically, you want to avoid being one about whom it is said, "He or she has a superb technique, but so cold. . . ." Or conversely, the equally discouraging, "He or she has such fire and drama and such depth of interpretation. Perhaps with a little training he or she could become a great artist."

At this point we have ascended to the highest level in balance, the cantus lībrātus. Perhaps we could treat this level of balance as a gestalt notion: all vocal, interpretive, and textual elements in balance with all emotional, intellectual, and spiritual components in the performance. This is a balance between the individual performer's *je ne sais quoi* and the collective soul; between that performer and his audience. It is this subjective harmony that finds its sympathetic chords in the hearts and souls of the listeners.

Now you have developed your technique from the simplest posture and breathing skill to the lofty cantus lībrātus. But how does all this theory translate itself into practical music making? In short, we have a technique and an ideal, but no program for working up a program.

I would like to offer as a final "coda" to this study in vocal development some guidelines for the preparation of a piece for performance—"practicing" in its original sense. These guidelines are rooted in my experience with the European system, a method involving three steps: *correpetition, coaching,* and *ensemble.*

In the first stage, called *Correpetition,* the singer attacks all the basics of score learning and diction. At this stage he or she practices only the notes of the melody (with piano, if necessary), in medium to light adjustment, at a reduced tempo, on *lu* (if the piece is lyric) or *da* (if it is not). At the same time, paralleling this work, the singer will isolate the text and practice it separately from the music. For articulation exercise, whisper the text. For vowel practice, sing through the entire piece on vowels only. For legato practice, sing through the entire piece sostenuto on one note using the text as written.

Then, when both "halves" of this exercise are perfected separately, the singer can move on to balancing the two together. During this phase he or she will sing the music with text slowly, as written, in a half-voice known among professionals as *marking* (a way of pacing the voice during strenuous rehearsals). At this point our vocalist dissects and drills the entire piece for problems in breathing, registration, and resonation.

The next stage in practicing is known as *coaching*. A coach is a teacher-professional who will review with the singer both poetic and musical aspects of interpretation. He or she will guide the singer to a clearer understanding of the composer's intentions regarding formal and historical requisites, artistic nuances and traditions, and dramatic ideas. If the singer is fortunate, he or she may also be able to visit a diction coach at this stage, a teacher who can help in the refinement of pronunciation and enunciation.

(May I interject a word about professional etiquette here: Never visit any coach until you are absolutely finished with the correpetition stage. Otherwise you are making strenuous demands on your coach, and such actions not only reflect badly on your musicianship but are insulting to the coach. In other words, do your own homework.)

The third stage in practicing is the ensemble "dress rehearsal" stage. Think of this stage as the perfecting of the balance between melody and accompaniment, and between statement and answer, musically. This stage involves the rehearsal of technical and interpretative facets of performance like dynamic balance; concurrence in nuances, tempi, phrasing, etc.; and "live performance" factors like acoustics of the hall, lighting, stage deportment, and so forth.

A crucial matter to be considered at this stage also is projection—not projection in the sense connected with resonation, but in the sense of role projection:

> An expert actor is a person who is able to communicate a great variety of thoughts, words, and emotional states to his audience. He accomplishes this by uttering words and by moving the muscles of his face, arms, and body. An expert opera singer is a person who, in addition to these skills, has a well-framed voice and a considerable knowledge of music.*

Once again, I think the best method for clarification is by example. And so, referring back to *Erlkönig*, follow this seven-staged expansion of the program for practicing, using the ballad as the piece to be learned.

---

*Boris Goldovsky, *Bringing Opera to Life* (Englewood Cliffs, N.J.: Prentice-Hall, 1968), p. 17. © 1968 by Prentice-Hall, Englewood Cliffs, N.J. Used by permission.

Step 1. Practice all vocal notes *mezzo-piano* on *lu*, (but don't undersing, losing ring). Practice all German vowels, then consonants. Then gently whisper the text. Put text and tone together, and balance.

Step 2. Practice the entire *Erlkönig* as a breathing exercise. Mark breathing spots, and practice posture-related skills such as vowel and consonant formation preceding inhalation. Practice long phrases (such as mm. 59 ff.) breath management and continuity of line. Practice legato two ways: (1) as written musically, on vowels alone; and (2) as written textually, on one tone sostenuto. Then bring into balance with articulation. Doublecheck for "gasps" in the rests, and review breathing at mm. 98 ff.

Step 3. Isolate potential registration problems (such as mm. 42 ff., with their leaps in and out of the passaggio). Check for control of the "cover" in passages such as mm. 98 ff.

Step 4. Test all vowels throughout as a resonation exercise, and for purity. This gesture must precede any vowel coloring and work on projection (in both senses). Determine if ring is present in the "chatty" section, mm. 88 ff.

Step 5. Take the text to a German coach. Correct any diction errors and practice nuances of enunciation. Then take your work to a vocal coach, after which you will synthesize his/her input with your seven-step plan of interpretation (Chapter 13).

Step 6. Practice all musical and interpretive facets together until polished and memorized. Bring music and poem into balance. Study the accompaniment.

Step 7. Work out ensemble problems with the accompanist (or conductor). Balance dynamics and phrasing, projection (in both senses), and legato, with accompaniment. Adjust to the acoustics of the hall. Repeat until there is a unity with voice, piano, and hall.

Now you are ready to perform! You have developed your technique and art in such a way that your cantus lībrātus is just what that concept implies: *your* singing. Your audience will be hearing your instrument and your interpretation. In this way you have developed what is called style, not an imitation of someone else.

In fact, style never obtains in the atmosphere of imitation. Style is born a priori in the soul of the artist; a posteriori imitation denies that birth, cheating the singer, who then can at best give us little more than a good reproduction. And who would choose a copy over an original?

There is an old Chinese proverb to that effect, which states, "If you would carve an ax handle, the model is in your hand."

One evening in the year 1928, the famed French singer Eva Gauthier was entertaining a small group of highly charged intellectuals. Among the guests were Maurice Ravel and his American admirer George Gershwin. The American version of the story goes that suddenly, out of the blue, Gershwin looked up from his habitual spot at the keyboard and squarely faced Ravel. Enthusiastically he proclaimed, "I would like to work with you."

Without so much as dropping an [ø], the older composer declined, adding, "Why should you be a second-rate 'Ravel' when you can be a first-rate 'Gershwin'?"*

You now have the means to be a "first-rate 'You.'" Your tone, your technique, your imagination—all come from within. Your interpretation and execution meet in the very stream which flows from above through your being to the soul of your audience.

There is no energy source, no generator behind your artistic current, however, if you imitate.

As you prepare to test this program on the real music world, at last, let these words—which direct my course—guide you always:

> *Neither a borrower or a lender be,*
> *For loan oft loses both itself and friend,*
> *And borrowing dulls the edge of husbandry.*
> *This above all, to thine own self be true.*

*This is admittedly a very free translation of the original episode. The French version retells the story as follows: "Vous pourriez perdre votre spontanéité mélodique et écriver de mauvais 'Ravel.'" (You would lose your melodic spontaneity and compose bad "Ravel."). In the context of this chapter, nonetheless, the American version conveys my message better.

Study Questions and Exercises

1. Take out the list you made at the start of the program. Make a similar assessment of your technique now, and compare the two. Comment on all areas of improvement, especially in posture and breathing. Periodically update this analysis, keeping it for those "rainy days" when you morosely doubt your improvement!

2. Review *all* Sieber exercises as a synthesis of habits. Select four of your favorites and relearn them for presentation in class, from memory. Use the seven-step plan of this chapter (even in the diction coaching, if possible) for your preparation. Critique as a class.

3. Choose a fresh piece for memorization and presentation in class. (If your piece is written in a foreign language, be sure to include a written translation with your presentation.) Study all interpretive as well as technical aspects. Utilize plans for both interpretive (Chapter 13) and technical (Chapter 14) preparation. Present—and tape—your piece in class.

International Phonetic Alphabet Symbols and Spellings

Vowels

[a]	as in *task*
[æ]	as in *cat*
[ɑ]	as in *father*
[ɒ]	as in *hot*
[ɔ]	as in *warm*
[e]	as in Ger. *Weh*
[ɛ]	as in *wed*
[ɜ]	as in *learn*
[ə]	as in *sofa*
[i]	as in *me*
[I]	as in *hit*
[y]	as in Fr. *une*
[Y]	as in Ger. *Müller*
[o]	as in *open*
[ø]	as in Ger. *böse*
[œ]	as in Ger. *Hölle*
[u]	as in *too*
[ʌ]	as in *tongue*
[U]	as in *took*

Consonants and Semi-Consonants

[b]	as in *bat*
[tʃ]	as in *check*
[d]	as in *dog*
[f]	as in *fit, rough*
[g]	as in *go*
[h]	as in *hope*
[hw]	as in *whether*
[d]	as in *joy*
[k]	as in *cool, take*
[l]	as in *look*
[m]	as in *seem*
[n]	as in *nice*
[ŋ]	as in *ring*
[p]	as in *pit*
[r]	as in *run*
[s]	as in *see*
[ʃ]	as in *sure*
[t]	as in *sit*
[θ]	as in *thin*

Consonants and Semi-Consonants
(continued)

[ð]   as in *this*

[v]   as in *eve*

[w]   as in *win*

[j]   as in *yet*

[z]   as in *zest*

[ʒ]   as in *vision*

Diphthongs

[aI]   as in *buy*
[əI]   as in *joy*
[ɛI]   as in *bay*
[Iɜ]   as in *fear*
[ɛɜ]   as in *fair*
[aɜ]   as in *far*
[əɜ]   as in *for*
[ɔɜ]   as in *pore*
[Uɜ]   as in *poor*
[au]   as in *now*
[ou]   as in *no*
[iu]   as in *beautiful*

Triphthongs

[aIɜ]   as in *tire*
[auɜ]   as in *tower*

Bibliography

Books

ADLER, KURT. *Phonetics and Diction in Singing.* Minneapolis: University of Minnesota Press, 1967.

ANDREAS, ESTHER, and ROBERT, M. FOWELLS. *The Voice of Singing.* New York: Carl Fischer, 1970.

BARTHOLOMEW, WILMER T. *Acoustics of Music.* New York: Prentice-Hall, 1945.

BERNAC, PIERRE. *The Interpretation of French Song.* New York: Praeger Publications, 1972.

BROWER, HARRIET. *Vocal Mastery.* New York: Frederick A. Stokes Co., 1920.

BROWN, RALPH M. *The Singing Voice.* New York: Macmillan, 1946.

BROWN, WILLIAM EARL, ed. *Vocal Wisdom: The Maxims of Giovanni Battista Lamperti,* 1931; rpt. New York: Arno Press, 1957.

COFFIN, BERTON. *Overtones of Bel Canto.* Metuchen, N.J.: The Scarecrow Press, 1980.

———, et al. *Phonetic Readings of Songs and Arias.* Boulder, Colorado: Pruett Press, 1964.

———. *The Sounds of Singing.* Boulder, Colorado: publ. author, 1976.

COLORNI, EVELINA. *Singers' Italian: A Manual of Diction and Phonetics.* New York: Schrimer Books, 1970.

COX, RICHARD G. *The Singer's Manual of German and French Diction.* New York: Schirmer Books, 1970.

DE YOUNG, RICHARD. *The Singer's Art: An Analysis of Vocal Principles.* Chicago: De Paul University Press, 1958.

DUEY, PHILIP A. *Bel Canto in Its Golden Age: A Study of Its Teaching Concepts.* New York: King's Crown Press, 1951.

ERROLLE, RALPH. *Italian Diction for Singers.* Boulder, Colorado: Pruett Press, 1963.

FIELDS, VICTOR ALEXANDER. *Training the Singing Voice.* New York: King's Crown Press, 1947.

FILLEBROWN, THOMAS. *Resonance in Singing and Speaking.* Philadelphia: Oliver Ditson Co., 1911.

FISCHER-DIESKAU, DIETRICH. *The Fischer-Dieskau Book of Lieder.* New York: Alfred A. Knopf, 1977.

GARCIA, MANUEL. *Hints on Singing.* Trans. Beata Garcia. New York: E. Schuberth and Co., 1894.

———. *New Treatise on the Art of Singing.* London: Leonard and Co., 18—.

GOLDOVSKY, BORIS. *Bringing Opera to Life.* New York: Appleton-Century-Crofts, 1968.

____, and ARTHUR SCHOEP. *Bringing Soprano Arias to Life.* New York: Schirmer Books, 1973.

GRUBB, THOMAS. *Singing in French.* New York: Schirmer Books, 1979.

HOWERTON, GEORGE. *Technique and Style in Choral Singing.* New York: Carl Fischer, 1957.

LARGE, JOHN W., ed. *Vocal Registers in Singing: Proceedings of the 78th Meeting of Acoustical Society of America, November 7, 1969, and Silver Jubilee Convention of NATS, December 28, 1969.* The Hague: Mouton and Co., 1973.

LEHMANN, LILLI. *How to Sing.* Trans. Richard Aldrich and Clara Willenbücher. New York: Macmillan, 1942.

LEHMANN, LOTTE. *More than Singing.* New York: Boosey and Hawkes, 1945.

MANCINI, GIOVANNI BATTISTA. *Practical Reflections on Figurative Singing.* Trans. Edward Foreman. Champaign, Illinois: Pro Musica Press, 1967.

MANÉN, LUCIE. *The Art of Singing: A Manual.* London: Faber Music, 1974.

MARCHESI, BLANCHE. *The Singer's Catechism and Creed.* London: J. M. Dent, 1932.

MARCHESI, MATHILDE. *Theoretical and Practical Vocal Method* New York: Dover Publications, 1970.

MARSHALL, MADELEINE. *The Singer's Manual of English Diction.* New York: Schirmer Books, 1953.

MORIARITY, JOHN. *Diction: Italian, Latin, French, German.* Boston: E.C. Schirmer Co., 1975.

ODOM, WILLIAM. *German for Singers.* New York: Schirmer Books, 1981.

PFAUTSCH, LLOYD. *English Diction for Singers.* New York: Lawson-Gould Music Publishers, 1971.

REID, CORNELIUS L. *Bel Canto, Principles and Practice.* New York: Coleman-Ross Co., 1950.

ROSE, ARNOLD. *The Singer and the Voice.* New York: St. Martin's Press, 1971.

ROSS, WILLIAM E. *Secrets of Singing.* Bloomington, Indiana: Ross, 1959.

SCHIØTZ, AKSEL. *The Singer and his Art.* London: Hamilton, 1970.

SHAKESPEARE, WILLIAM. *The Art of Singing.* London: Metzler and Co., 1893; rpt. Philadelphia: Presser, 1921.

SIEBER, FERDINAND. *36 Eight-Measure Exercises,* Opus 93. New York: G. Schirmer, 1967.

TETRAZZINI, LUISA. *How to Sing.* New York: George H. Doran Co., 1923.

TOSI, PIETRO FRANCESCO. *Observations on the Florid Song.* 1723; trans. J. E. Galliard, 1743; facs. rpt. New York: Johnson Reprint Corp., 1980.

URIS, DOROTHY. *To Sing in English.* New York: Boosey and Hawkes. 1971.

VENNARD, WILLIAM. *Singing: The Mechanism and the Technique.* New York: Carl Fischer, 1967.

WHITLOCK, WELDON. *Bel Canto for the Twentieth Century.* Milwaukee: Pro Musica Press, 1968.

WITHERSPOON, HERBERT. *Singing: A Treatise for Teachers and Students.* New York: G. Schirmer, 1925.

Articles

DELATTRE, PIERRE. "Vowel Color and Voice Quality." *NATS Bulletin* 15, no. 1 (Oct. 1958): 4.

HARPSTER, RICHARD W. "Concepts and Exercises in Choral Singing: A Paradigm for Practice." Monograph. (In review.)

———. "Genius in the Eighteenth Century: C. F. D. Schubart's *Vom musikalischen Genie. Current Musicology* 15 (1973): 73–77.

———. "Schumann's *Scenes from Goethe's Faust:* Some Guidelines for Interpretation and Performance." *The Choral Journal* 28, no. 6 (Feb. 1978), and 28, no. 7 (March 1978): 8–13; 14–17.

RASKIN, JUDITH. "American Bel Canto." *Opera News,* Jan. 15, 1966, p. 6.

RUTH, WILHELM. "The Registers of the Singing Voice." *NATS Bulletin* 19, no. 4 (May 1963): 2–5.

VAN DEN BERT, JANWILLEM, and WILLIAM VENNARD. "Toward an Objective Vocabulary for Voice Pedagogy. *NATS Bulletin* 15, no. 3 (February 15, 1959): 10–16.

VENNARD, WILLIAM. "Registration." *Music Journal* 45 (March 1959): 52–53.

Index